Spiritual Precautions

by Clay Sterrett

Extra copies and/or a listing of other materials may be obtained from:

CFC Literature
P.O. Box 245
Staunton, VA 24402-0245

ISBN 0-9621713-2-8
Printed in the United States of America

Contents

Introduction

Believers in our day are faced with spiritual dangers on every side: blatant immorality, secular humanism, unrestrained materialism, lukewarmness in the church, and counterfeit religion. Much has been written and said about these dangers, but often lacking is an emphasis on practical, preventive safeguards which will keep God's people safe and sound in the faith.

In an earlier work, Safeguards for the Saints, my focus was upon seven essential, but often neglected, truths for the body of Christ. I compared these truths to "roadsigns" along a narrow road which, if applied, would keep believers safe from many dangers and point them in the right direction. In this subsequent volume, seven additional truths are shared which are equally essential to the spiritual health of any individual and church family.

The seven topics in Spiritual Precautions may not be very popular titles in the body of Christ. By this I mean there seem to currently be little interest and certainly little in print about these subjects. However, I think the importance of these titles goes much beyond my own personal preference; I believe they are foundational in resolving the majority of personal problems believers encounter, whether they be strife in the church, disharmony in a family, or internal difficulties. The application of these realities can mean the difference between a mere outward form of religion and a living faith that results in Christ-like character.

Following are the seven precautions in this volume:

1. Showing Mercy to All Men

2. Keeping a Listening Ear

3. Responding in Meekness

4. Bearing Our Cross Daily

5. Ordering Our Lives Before the Lord

6. Giving Room to the Holy Spirit

7. Maintaining Hope for the Future

Every Christian, whether a new believer or a veteran saint, will find these truths vital to his successful walk with Christ. These topics will not be "new" truths to most readers, but they are concepts which need to be continually written on our hearts and minds. I can echo the words of Paul:

> *For myself I feel certain that you, my brothers, have real Christian character and experience, and that you are capable of keeping each other on the right road. Nevertheless I have in some places written to you with a greater frankness, to refresh your minds with truths that you already know.*[1]

My suggestion in reading Spiritual Precautions is to read it over a seven day period, taking one chapter a day to prayerfully consider. I have tried to avoid being "wordy" and kept a primary emphasis on the Scripture itself, which speaks so much more clearly than any human teacher. One other suggestion: in each chapter ask the Lord to make personally applicable at least two verses which you can meditate upon now and in the days to come.

My prayer is that God, through the Holy Spirit, will give greater revelation of who we really are and what His provision is in Christ. We can be thankful Jesus cares deeply for our spiritual welfare, and He is *able to keep you from falling.*[2] Let us humbly welcome "the finger of God" to point out any deficiencies we have, and receive His grace to make the necessary adjustments, so in That Day we may stand unashamed, having no regrets over what might have been different in our lives.

NOTES

1.Rom. 15:14-15 Phillips

2.Jude 24

Chapter One

Showing Mercy To All Men

During the Napoleonic Wars, a young, battle-weary French soldier fell asleep while on guard duty. He was court-martialed, found guilty, and sentenced to death. His widowed mother somehow arranged an audience with the Emperor Napoleon himself. Falling prostrate at his feet, she begged for her son's life to be spared, explaining he was her only child and her sole means of support. Napoleon grew weary of her pleas. "Madam, your son does not deserve mercy. He deserves to die," he said coldly. To which the mother immediately replied, "Of course, sire, you are right. That's why I am asking you to show mercy on him. If he were so deserving, it wouldn't be mercy." Napoleon was so touched by the logic of her statement that he pardoned the soldier.[1]

There is no other word quite like mercy. Mercy is a unique quality that originates from God and should distinguish the people of God. Even the ungodly will take notice of this attribute:

"Look, we have heard that the kings of the house of Israel are merciful..."[2]

Both in the Old Covenant and the New Covenant, mercy is in God's "top three" priority list; it is an indispensable trait that needs to be in the life of every believer:

He has showed you, O man, what is good. And what does the LORD require of you? To act justly and to love mercy and to walk humbly with your God. (Micah 6:8)

"Woe to you...you hypocrites! You have neglected the more important matters of the law--justice, mercy and faithfulness." (Matthew 23:23)

Probably none of us on this side of eternity will ever fully appreciate the mercy of God. Charles Spurgeon once said, "All the world tastes of his sparing mercy, those who hear of the gospel partake of his inviting mercy, the saints live by his saving mercy, are preserved by his upholding mercy, are cheered by his consoling mercy, and will enter heaven through his infinite and everlasting mercy."[3]

The Hebrew word for mercy (HESED) is a word so full of richness that no one English term can translate it. Different translations include "compassion"(KJ), "great love" (NIV), "steadfast love"(RSV), and "kindness." HESED is the word used for covenant loyalty. It is a love often demonstrated very practically to those in need. Mercy is different from grace in that grace looks upon men in their sin while mercy looks upon men in their misery.[4] In other words, grace is the remedy for sin itself; mercy is the remedy for the consequences of sin. Grace brings forgiveness; mercy brings compassion and care as well. This is best pictured in the story of the Good Samaritan.

In this story a true neighbor is seen in the Samaritan who shows practical care for a man who has been beaten by robbers and then neglected by two religious leaders. The Samaritan is never called "good" by Jesus; he was nothing special -- just a man who was willing to walk on a different side of the road to get involved. When asked the question, "Which of the three who passed by was a true neighbor?" the proper answer comes: *The one who had mercy on him.*[5] J.B. Phillips translates the verse: *The one who gave him practical sympathy.*[6]

Mercy involves a giving of oneself to another when there is no obligation to give. God did not have to provide a coat of skins for Adam and Eve to cover their nakedness. God did not have to brand Cain to spare his life. God did not have to wait over a thousand years to send the flood to destroy vile and wicked men. God did not have to rescue Lot out of Sodom before it was consumed by heaven-sent fire. God did not have to pardon King David's great sin of adultery with Bathsheba. God did not have to bring His people out of Babylonian captivity and restore them to their land. God did not have to restrain His hand when boastful men nailed the hands of His precious Son to a cross.

There is abundant evidence of the mercy of God. How can a slothful man abuse his body with alcoholic drink, smoking, and no exercise, and yet live to be eighty? Why do homosexuals who contract AIDS sometimes live seven more years? Is not this evidence of a most merciful Father, who graciously gives time for all of us to realize His great love? *He has no wish that any man should be destroyed; he wishes that all men should find the way to repentance.*[7]

Better Than We Deserve

As illustrated in our opening story, mercy also means treating an offender better than he deserves. This is further illustrated in the story in which the Arameans, enemies of Israel, tried to capture Elisha (II Kings 6). As the enemy approached, God answered Elisha's specific prayer by striking the entire Aramean army blind. Elisha then led this helpless army, unknowingly to them, directly into Samaria, the capital city of Northern Israel. The response of Elisha and the Israeli king stand out in stark contrast to the torturous methods of their contemporaries:

> *When the king of Israel saw them, he asked Elisha, "Shall I kill them, my father? Shall I kill them?"*
>
> *"Do not kill them," he answered. "Would you kill men you have captured with your own sword or bow? Set food and water before them so that they may eat and drink and then go back to their master." So he prepared a great feast for them, and after they had finished eating and drinking, he sent them away, and they returned to their master. So the bands from Aram stopped raiding Israel's territory.*[8]

Mercy is for the <u>undeserving</u>, not the deserving. If we ever feel undeserving of God's goodness toward us, then we need to better appreciate His mercy. In giving a brief history of Israel, in one chapter Nehemiah describes their disobedience, rebellion, stubbornness, murder of the prophets, and continual evil actions even after God graciously delivered them from their enemies (see Neh. 9). Despite all of this, however, their chapter in history concludes with these wonderful words:

> *But in your great mercy you did not put an end to them or abandon them, for you are a gracious and merciful God.*[9]

One fact is certain -- if God dealt with any of us as our sins deserve, WE WOULD NOT STAND A CHANCE! God is righteous and He becomes angry at sin; one day we will all stand before His judgment seat. The following passage, however, puts things in perspective:

> *The LORD is merciful and gracious, slow to anger, and abounding in mercy. He will not always strive with us, nor will He keep his anger forever; He has not dealt with us according to our sins, nor punished us according to our iniquities. For as the heavens are high above the earth, so great is His mercy toward those who fear Him.*[10]

The Height of God's Mercy

The loftiness of God's mercy is seen in *the mercy seat,* which was part of the ark of the covenant in the tabernacle. For over five hundred years the tabernacle was the center of worship for the people of God. Inside this modest tent, the high priest would enter once a year into a small room, the Holy of Holies, on The Day of Atonement and sprinkle blood for the sins of the people.[11] The ark of the covenant is where this activity took place. It represented the presence and power of God Himself. The ark, a wooden box covered inside and out with pure gold, contained the stone tablets, the ten commandments given to Moses. No man, past or present, ever kept the righteous requirements of those laws. The commandments have always produced an awareness of how sinful we are -- how far short we fall apart from the intervention of Christ.[12]

On top of this box was a gold slab called *the mercy seat*[13] or *the atonement cover*[14] which stood between two sculptured gold cherubim. The mercy seat was where God spoke to Moses[15], and it is the place where God meets us today. Whenever God's people fell short of their covenant obligations by sinning against God and breaking His holy commands, the blood of the sacrifice sprinkled on the mercy seat made atonement for their sin and reconciled them to God. Today, when we fall short and guilt floods our souls, the mercy seat is still available as we come to Jesus, our mediator of a new and better covenant.[16]

In the mercy seat we see the immeasurable greatness of God's mercy. Every item in the tabernacle had specific measurements for all its facets. The mercy seat had specific measurements given by the Lord for its width and length[17], but no dimension is given for its heighth. Hallelujah! This describes the unlimited mercy of God: *for as high as the heavens are above the earth so great is His mercy toward them that fear Him.*[18]

God is not stingy with His mercy; He is ready to forgive and *plenteous in mercy* toward any who call on His name.[19] He is rich in mercy, quick in mercy, and abounding in mercy. His mercy is vast, from *everlasting to everlasting* to those who fear him and keep His covenant.[20] Probably to remind us just how far his mercy goes, God gave us Psalm 136. Here is just a portion:

> *Oh, give thanks to the LORD, for He is good.*
> *For His mercy endures forever.*
> *Oh, give thanks to the God of gods.*
> *For His mercy endures forever.*
> *Oh, give thanks to the Lord of lords:*
> *For His mercy endures forever.*[21]

This phrase, *For His mercy endures forever,* is repeated twenty-six times in this one psalm! Our God, who has no room for "vain repetitions," is making a statement that needs to be eternally inscribed on our hearts: IF WE HAVE ANYTHING AT ALL,

IT'S BY HIS MERCY! Knowing the mercy of God will keep us both thankful and humble. We need to continually come to the place where we utterly depend upon His mercy for our past salvation and present security:

> *It is of the Lord's mercies that we are not consumed, because his compassions fail not.*[22]

> *He saved us, not because of righteous things we had done, but because of his mercy...*[23]

To Whom Does God Show Mercy?

Those who are recipients of the mercy of God might surprise us; God in His word declares, *I will have mercy on whom I have mercy.*[24] Sometimes people whom we think are the least "worthy" of the mercy of God receive it, even abundantly! Paul received mercy even though he was *a blasphemer, a persecutor, and a violent man.*[25] I heard of a recent tragedy when a hurricane hit the North Carolina coast. A group in a particular house had been talking that night about Christ and one lady was very antagonistic, even mocking the Christian faith as her believing friends were trying to convince her. When the hurricane hit, this house was destroyed and only one life was spared. Guess who? Yes, the antagonistic lady. That's mercy!

We can neither predict nor pinpoint recipients, but Scripture does indicate certain types of people will especially receive the mercy of God:

1. Those who are humble.

Jesus told a story of two men who both went to the temple to pray. One was a very self-centered religious man who was condescending toward other men: *God, I thank you that I am not like all other men -- robbers, evildoers, adulterers -- or even like this tax collector.*[26] The other man, an unpopular tax collector, was a humble man; his prayer was simply, *God, have mercy on me, a sinner.*[27] It was the tax collector who received the Lord's favor and mercy. God always resists the proud, but showers his grace and mercy on those who humble themselves.[28]

2. Those who confess and forsake their sins.

Throughout the Bible we see that those believers who try to hide their sin receive the judgment of God. (Two good examples of this are Achan in the Old Testament[29] and Ananias and Sapphira in the New Testament.[30]) On the other hand, believers who face up to and forsake their sins find the mercy of God. (Two good examples of this are King David in O.T.[31] and Peter in N.T.[32]) Our excuses and explanations will hinder the mercy of God; repentance and confession are what's needed:

> *Let the wicked forsake his way,*
> *And the unrighteous man his thoughts;*
> *Let him return to the Lord,*
> *And He will have mercy on him;*
> *And to our God,*
> *For He will abundantly pardon.*[33]

> *He who conceals his sins does not prosper, but*
> *whoever confesses and renounces them finds mercy.*[34]

3. Those who have persistent, shameless faith.

There is something about persistent, unrelenting faith that touches the heart of God. The widow in Jesus' parable kept pestering the unrighteous judge until he granted her what she requested. This illustrates the way our Righteous Judge will grant mercy and justice to those who *cry out to Him day and night.*[35]

Another example of persistent faith is in the story of blind Bartimaeus who even became a little "undignified" in yelling for Jesus to stop and help him:

> *As Jesus and his disciples, together with a large crowd, were leaving the city, a blind man, Bartimaeus (that is, the Son of Timaeus), was sitting by the roadside begging. When he heard that it was Jesus of Nazareth, he began to shout, "Jesus, Son of David, have mercy on me!" Many rebuked him and told him to be quiet, but he shouted all the more, "Son of David, have mercy on me!"*[36]

Bartimaeus not only received the Master's attention, but he also received his request --his sight restored. Persistent, shameless faith still gets the Master's attention today.

4. Those who are His afflicted people.

When God's people are afflicted, it moves His heart to mercy and compassion. Corrie Ten Boom once related an experience of being in a cold, damp prison cell in which she had to sleep on a stone floor. One especially cold night, as she talked to her Heavenly Father about it, a gust of warm air began blowing across the floor and continued through the night. That's the mercy of God. Someone has defined mercy as "God's ministry to the miserable."

When God's people suffered in Egypt under Pharaoh's cruel hand, it did not escape the attention of God: *I have surely seen the affliction of My people who are in Egypt...I am aware of their sufferings. So I have come down to deliver them...*[37] King

David was also aware of God's concern: *Thou hast seen my affliction; Thou hast known the troubles of my soul...*[38] For any one of us who is presently facing affliction, we have a sure promise:

> *The Lord has comforted His people, and will have mercy on His afflicted..."I will not forget you. See, I have inscribed you on the palm of my hands."*[39]

5. Those who work hard for the Lord.

Hard-working servants of God especially seem to enjoy the mercy of God. We see this in the lives of three fellow-workers of Paul, the apostle. Epaphroditus, a close friend of Paul's, almost died because he worked so hard for the Lord, but *God had mercy on him.*[40] Another special comrade of Paul's was Onesiphorus, one of the few men who stuck with Paul after he was imprisoned. Paul was most grateful to this friend and said of him, *He often refreshed me...May the Lord grant that he will find mercy from the Lord on that day!*[41] A third special friend, Timothy, also was a recipient of the mercy of God. In thirteen letters Paul wrote, he always begins with the two words, *Grace and peace to you from God the Father and the Lord Jesus Christ...* In writing the two letters to Timothy, however, his introduction changes as a third term is inserted: *Grace, mercy, and peace from God the Father...*[42] As a young man who was exhorted by his "father-in-the-faith" to excel in zeal and good works, possibly Paul knew Timothy would need a special measure of mercy as well.

Those who work hard for the Lord, being led by His Spirit, sometimes pay a price in their own personal interests, family life, and health. One factor, however, that compensates for the cost is an extra measure of the mercy of God.

The Importance of Our Showing Mercy

Jesus told a story of a servant who had been forgiven many debts, equivalent to several million dollars, by a gracious king. This servant, however, when he found a fellow-servant who owed him just a few dollars, was very hard and threw him into prison, despite his pleas. When this report reached the king, he was furious, and called the first servant in:

> *"You wicked servant," he said, "I canceled all that debt of yours because you begged me to. Shouldn't you have had mercy on your fellow servant just as I had on you?" In anger his master turned him over to the jailers to be tortured, until he should pay back all he owed. This is how my heavenly Father will treat each of you unless you forgive your brother from your heart.*[43]

We cannot underestimate the importance of having a merciful heart, even to those who do not deserve our mercy. The fact is --we have a gracious King who has been extremely merciful to us. Can we dare not show mercy to our fellow servants? If we withhold mercy, the Master will hand us over to "the torturers." I believe this means that those who have unmerciful and unforgiving hearts subject themselves to demonic forces. The word in Greek for "jailers" not only refers to jailers who keep people in bondage, but torturers who use the rack to get the truth. Whatever conclusions we may draw from this, it should be an encouragement to *be merciful, just as your Father is merciful.*[44]

Mercy Must be Joined with Truth

Those who are merciful have a sure promise: *they will be shown mercy.*[45] Being merciful does not imply we avoid judging and dealing with sin in the body of Christ; at least three times in Scripture we see the two words "mercy and truth" joined together.[46] No Christian can afford to be without either of these. Without truth we tend only to be sympathetic and look at needs from our own human perspective, rather than God's larger view. Without mercy, on the other hand, we become too hard and legalistic. Technically we may be right, but we have the wrong spirit. Jesus had the right balance. When a woman was caught in adultery, Jesus showed mercy (*Neither do I condemn you*), but He also spoke truth (*Go now and leave your life of sin.*[47]) If a drug addict or homosexual comes into our assembly, we should welcome him and have genuine concern. If he is convicted of sin, however, and chooses to follow Christ, he must be encouraged to sever former ties and "sin no more." A man like this will need a good combination of mercy and truth.

Possibly between judgment and mercy we should chose to be "heavier" on the side of mercy: *mercy triumphs over judgment!*[48] One translation puts it in practical terms: *The man who makes no allowances for others will find none made for him.*[49] This should encourage all of us to be a little more merciful!

NOTES

1.David Seamands, Healing Grace (Victor Books, Wheaton, IL, 1988) p. 111

2.I Kings. 20:31

3.Charles Spurgeon, Treasury of David, Vol. 2 (Hendrickson Publishers, Peabody, MA) p.279

4.see Richard Trench, Synonyms of the New Testament (Eerdmans, Grand Rapids, MI,1953) p.169

5.Lk. 10:37

6.Lk. 10:37 Phillips

7.II Pet. 3:9 Phillips

8.II Kings 6:21-23

9.Neh. 9:21

10.Psa. 103:8-11 NKJV

11.see Lev. 16

12.Rom. 3:20; 7:7-12

13.see Heb. 9:5 KJ where it is called "the mercy seat." This Greek word means "a propitiation, a means of appeasing or expiating" (Thayer). The Greek word is only used here and Rom. 3:25 where it is called "a sacrifice of atonement" (NIV).

14.Lev. 16:2. In the Septuagint (Greek O.T.) same word is used here as in the references in the above footnote.

15.Num. 7:89 KJ

16.Heb. 9:11-15

17.Ex. 25:17

18.Psa. 103:11 KJ

19.Psa. 86:5

20.Psa. 103:17

21.Psa. 136:1-3 NKJV

22.Lam. 3:22 KJ

23.Tit. 3:5

24.Rom. 9:15

25.I Tim. 1:13

26.Lk. 18:11
27.Lk. 18:12
28.I Pet. 5:5
29.Joshua 7
30.Acts 5:1-11
31.II Sam. 12:13; Psa. 51
32.Jn. 18:15-27;21:15-19
33.Is. 55:7 NKJV
34.Prov. 28:13
35.Lk. 18:7
36.Mk. 10:46-49
37.Ex. 3:7 NAS
38.Psa. 31:7 NAS
39.Is. 49:13-16
40.Phil 2:25-30
41.II Tim. 1:16-18
42.I Tim. 1:2; II Tim. 1:2
43.Matt. 18:23-35
44.Lk. 6:36
45.Matt. 5:7
46.Psa. 25:10 KJ; Psa. 85:10 KJ and Prov. 3:3 KJ
47.Jn. 8:11
48.James 2:13
49.James 2:13 Phillips

Chapter Two

Keeping A Listening Ear

The Civil War probably was the most devastating experience our country has ever endured. For over four years our nation was split into two factions -- north and south, with sometimes in the same family brother fighting against brother. More American lives were lost in this war than in any other war in our history. It is hard to comprehend what it must have been like to live in a split nation for four long years. Can you imagine, however, what it would be like to be a citizen in a country that was split for 325 years ?! This happened to Israel beginning about 931 B.C., shortly after the reign of King David, and it was initiated when one man failed to have a listening ear.

David's son Solomon had not been the same caliber of king as his father David. In his last years Solomon gave himself to selfish pursuits of luxury and happiness, and as a result, the best interests of the people were forgotten and the kingdom was almost wrecked. When he died and his son, Rehoboam, took over the throne, tensions still existed from Solomon's neglect of and hardness toward the people. Rehoboam was approached by the elders of Israel, who appealed to him to lighten the "heavy yoke" and harsh labor Solomon had put on them. After considering the request for three days, Rehoboam made his tragic mistake:

> *But Rehoboam rejected the advice the elders gave him and consulted the young men who had grown up with him and were serving him...So the king did not listen to the people...*[1]

After Rehoboam accepted this bad advice and took an even harsher approach, a lot of the Israelites rebelled against him, and as a result, the nation split into two factions: Judah in the south and Israel in the north, a split that would not be healed for 325 years. God had ordained this event because of Solomon's idolatry[2], but it was a king refusing to correctly listen that initiated the crisis.

Few of us realize how crucial it is to have a listening ear; our spiritual well-being may depend upon it:

> *If you listen carefully to the voice of the LORD your God and do what is right in his eyes...I will not bring on you any of the diseases I brought on the Egyptians...*[3]

> *But it shall come about, if you will not listen to the voice of the Lord your God...that all these curses shall come upon you and overtake you.*[4]

Our Problem With Talkativeness

Effective listening is one of our most neglected arts. Most high schools and colleges teach courses in public speaking. Most seminaries and Bible schools require courses in Homiletics (i.e. How to Preach Effectively). How often, however, have we heard of a course entitled, "Effective Listening?"

Scripture says *everyone should be quick to listen, slow to speak.*[5] If someone is overeager to speak, *there will be more hope for a fool than for him.*[6] Jesus often exhorted those who listened to have *ears to hear.*[7] As disciples of Jesus we should *listen as a disciple.*[8] We need to restrain our words and quiet our spirits to listen more effectively. Bill Gothard, who has counseled thousands of teenagers, says the number one complaint teens speak about is that their fathers do not take the time to really listen to them.

How do we know if we have this problem? We can know if we are bad listeners if we...

> ...keep on looking at the newspaper when our wife is speaking to us.
> ...glance around the room when someone tells a story <u>we</u> are not interested in.
> ...cannot hear a brother share without immediately adding some of <u>our</u> insight.

The root cause of talkativeness is <u>self</u> -- we want to express <u>our</u> opinions more than we want to receive from others:

> *A fool finds no pleasure in understanding but delights in airing his own opinions.*[9]

A fool's pride makes him talk too much...[10]

Let the wise listen and add to their learning...[11]

Paul Billheimer says, "Pride of opinion in nonessentials...is the worst form of sin -- it is idolatry...To sacrifice one's opinions requires a humility strange to most of us."[12] When we have pride of opinion, we enjoy having people listen to us and/or we try to force them to go our way. Watchman Nee shares this word of exhortation:

> Never consider it to be too good a thing that people listen to you...You may take delight in making your idea and opinion the direction and light of other people. Let it be clearly acknowledged by you that your idea is not to be the direction of others, nor your opinion to be their light. Humbly learn not to drag people along your way, nor to pressure them to follow you or even to obey the Lord. If brothers and sisters are willing to walk with you, thank God. But when they want to choose their own way, let them so choose...One true characteristic of a man who knows God is that he has no thought of forcing people to listen to or follow him.[13]

The Importance of Listening to the Lord

Listening to the Lord is a lifetime lesson for the Christian. Our society is so hectic and fast-paced that it is difficult for Christians to settle down and take time to listen to God. God's cry from old has always been the same: *Oh, that my people would listen to me...*[14]

We are called to be bond-servants of the Lord. In the Old Testament, there was one visible mark of those who chose to give up their freedom and become bond-servants of a master -- a pierced ear.[15] Of all the parts of the body, why was the ear chosen? Lance Lambert explains:

> Service does not begin with hands nor with feet but with the ear. A servant may be a Mister Superman -- strong, healthy, able -- but if he can't hear, what is the use? I say to him, "Come here." What is the point of having a servant if he doesn't come?...If I tell him to cook the meal, but he cannot hear and he goes on doing his own thing, what good is he to me? What is the use of a servant who cannot hear?[16]

Many of us simply do not know how to just be silent and listen; in the home we keep a television going, in the car the radio blares, and even when jogging we listen to a portable radio/tapeplayer. Our Lord spoke the following words to His church:

> *If anyone listens to my voice and opens the door, I will go into his house and dine with him, and he with me.*[17]

This verse is usually used by evangelicals for sinners who need salvation; however, it is addressed to believers who have left the Lord outside. We can become so absorbed with our own lives that the Lord gets left out. This is illustrated in this story of a medical doctor. After attending his own pastor for six months, the doctor felt led to say to him, "Pastor, you've been a busy man. It may be that God has something to say to you, but you were too busy to listen, so He has had to lay you on your back that you might hear His voice.

As the doctor was leaving the house, these same words suddenly struck him. He himself was a busy man--far too busy--and did not give much time to listening to the voice of God. Immediately he determined to practice what he had preached to his pastor. "And from that day," he said, "I have sat at the close of each day for an hour in the quiet of my study. Not to speak to God, but to listen to what He might say to me, and to lay the whole day's work open to his gaze."[18]

We should not presume upon God; His voice is not just automatically heard -- we must learn to be quiet before Him. Elijah discovered this; he found the Lord was not in a mighty rushing wind, not in a great shaking, not in a fire, but the Lord was only to be found *in a gentle whisper.*[19] When Jesus was gloriously transfigured, His face shone like the sun, and Elijah and Moses appeared, talking with Him. When Peter woke up he became excited and like many church people started talking about a building program: *I will put up three shelters --one for you, one for Moses and one for Elijah!* Before Peter could even finish talking, the Heavenly Father interrupted him and said, "*This is My beloved Son...listen to Him!*"[20]

Listening to the Lord Continually

Our active faith can quickly degenerate into mere routine or tradition. This is indeed one of our greatest dangers, for it is then that we fail to hear God's voice. Tradition can cause God's living word to become *of none effect.*[21] One Biblical author, in recording an overview of Israel's history, ends with these pathetic words: *However, they did not listen, but they did according to their earlier custom.*[22]

Joshua was a man of faith who wholeheartedly followed the Lord. However, he got in trouble and compromised with the enemy when he failed to seek God's voice continually: *The men of Israel sampled their provisions but did not inquire of the LORD.*[23] DeVern Fromke shares his concern for the body of Christ:

> I am alarmed! Many in this hour, even among God's choice servants, have heard God speak in the past; but they have not had a fresh word for a long time. We need to be concerned when hearing is not continuous. When messages sound like an experience from the past, we need to be alarmed. Above all we need to be tuned in to what God is saying NOW, as His present truth for this hour.[24]

We do not learn to listen to the Lord by reading a book about it or taking a seminar in "How to Listen to God"; it is a habit to be learned. As Brother Lawrence says, we need to "practice the presence of God." Our relationship with the Lord is often compared in Scripture to that of a shepherd and his sheep. A sheep learns to hear his master's voice. Eastern shepherds often give individual names to their sheep and talk to them like we do to dogs and cats. Several flocks of sheep can be separated when the individual shepherd calls his sheep. Jesus says, *The sheep which are mine are in the habit of listening to my voice.*[25]

The more we learn to listen to God, the more He can entrust to us. Listening will open our hearts and lead to further revelation from God. It is recorded of the wealthy saleswoman, Lydia, who heard the word of God through Paul: *as she listened to us, the Lord opened her heart and she accepted all that Paul was saying.*[26]The boy Samuel was only used to hearing the voice of men, but he grew to listen to the voice of God: *And Samuel said, "Speak, Lord, for your servant is listening..."*[27]

God has much to tell us if we take time to listen. May we grow to hear His voice as He speaks personally to us: *Listen and hear My voice; pay attention and hear what I say.*[28]

The Importance of Listening to Our Families

We often have the hardest time hearing those who are closest to us --our parents, parents-in-law, mates and children. Scripture tells us:

> *Listen to your father who begot you, and do not despise your mother when she is old.*[29]

God's word never tells us to quit listening to parents and in-laws after we meet Christ. In fact a blessing is promised to those who continue to *honor their parents*.[30] To "honor" means to "value and esteem highly"; it means we have a respectful attitude and maintain a listening ear when they speak. Moses had this proper attitude toward his father-in-law Jethro, who gave him advice about selecting additional leaders to assist him: *So Moses listened to his father-in-law and did all that he said.*[31] Even if parents and in-laws are not Christians, they still may have some wisdom and even a word from the Lord to us. This is not to imply, however, that we swallow everything they say. We should always take advice like we eat chicken --eat the good and spit out the bones! Scripture says, *Test everything. Hold on to the good!*[32]

We also need to listen respectfully to our mates. Some husbands will listen to certain "experts" but fail miserably to listen to their own wives. A good example of this is Pilate, who listened to all the religious leaders, but failed to hear his wife's exhortations.[33] A wife will often see many practical details that a husband is blinded to, and if he is not receptive to her advice, he will miss out. For example, a wife may have a suggestion about the way a husband dresses. If he is stubborn and proud, he will dismiss her suggestions or make light of them. After a while, the wife will quit trying to be helpful, and will just let him dress as he pleases. I have learned over the years, sometimes the hard way, that when my wife gives advice, I need to pay attention! If I don't welcome her advice, I will miss an important safeguard God has given me.

The Importance of Listening to Fellow Christians

This is an area where some Christians really get in trouble. Some would like to listen to God directly, but prefer not to listen to other Christians; rather they limit God's speaking through their study of the word, or their personal communion with God. It is an amazing truth, however, that how well we listen to fellow Christians may determine how well we listen to the Lord. A failure to listen is one chief reason some have been deceived by the "spirit of falsehood."

> *We are from God, and whoever knows God listens to us; but whoever is not from God does not listen to us. This is how we recognize the Spirit of truth and the spirit of falsehood.*[34]

When Jesus sent out his original disciples, how people received their message was directly related to how well they received the Lord Himself:

> *"He who listens to you listens to me; he who rejects you rejects me...*[35]

The input and reproof of Christians is something we need and should welcome. Even if it is not entirely accurate, any reproof should be carefully and humbly considered. This is not to say we need to listen to a gossip or continual pessimist. We need to have, however, an approachable spirit:

> *He who refuses correction is his own worst enemy,*
> *but he who listens to reproof learns sense.*[36]

A. W. Tozer encourages an "open spirit" when folks bring criticism:

> Don't defend your church or your organization against criticism. If the criticism is false it can do no harm. If it is true you need to hear it and do something about it.[37]

The Even Greater Importance of Listening to the Church

> *But if he will not listen, take one or two others along, so that every matter may be established by the testimony of two or three witnesses. If he refuses to listen to them, tell it to the church; and if he refuses to listen even to the church, treat him as you would a pagan or a tax collector.*[38]

This verse should cause us all to walk more humbly. If several brothers ever come to us about a concern, we should listen carefully and respectfully. If we fail to listen to a legitimate concern, the Scripture says we are to be considered as a "pagan" or "tax collector." Listening to a body of believers is serious business.

The elders (pastors) of a local church are God's delegated authorities. They are human, they make mistakes, they do not hear the Lord perfectly, but nonetheless, they are God's delegated authorities. This is not to say we are never to question or blindly obey men, especially if advice is given that is contrary to Scripture.[39] In Old Testament times, one's attitude in listening to leaders was a serious matter:

> *And the man who acts presumptuously by not listening to the priest who stands there to serve the Lord your God, nor to the judge, that man should die; thus you shall purge the evil from Israel. Then all the people will hear...*[40]

Let us be thankful we are living under a new covenant of mercy and grace. The principles, however, hold true: it is crucial to listen when several brothers speak to us, especially if they are the leaders of our local church. A listening ear is an indispensable safeguard for our spiritual well-being.

How To Become An Effective Listener

1. Welcome new information and advice from others.

> *A poor, yet wise lad is better than an old and foolish king who no longer knows how to receive instruction.*[41]

If we ever think we are becoming very "learned" in the Christian faith, we're in trouble. A believer who thinks there are only a few people from whom he can learn is not a wise man; he is rightly called a "fool" by Scripture: *A fool thinks he needs no advice, but a wise man listens to others.*[42]

There is no place for "know-it-all-Christians"; a willingness to be taught is a key to learning from the Lord:

> *To learn you must want to be taught...*[43]

> *Get all the advice you can and be wise the rest of your life.*[44]

2. Do not be too particular to whom you listen.

One of the most subtle dangers is we become selective in listening, i.e. we limit our listening to only a few people who are telling us what we want to hear. This is what the Bible calls "itching ears."

> *For the time will come when men will not put up with sound doctrine. Instead, to suit their own desires, they will gather around them a great number of teachers to say what their itching ears want to hear.*[45]

How can we tell if we have "itching ears?" Here are a few indicators:

- we move from church to church when someone says something we do not like.
- we can only listen to a few select men who "really teach the word."
- we are always seeking a "new revelation" and complain frequently, "I've heard all that before."

Jesus is our model example of a good listener. As a young boy he did not go around telling everyone who He was and what He thought they needed to hear; instead He listened.

When His parents found Him with the teachers of the temple, He was *both listening to them and asking them questions.*[46]

We should be ready to listen to anyone. God may speak to us through an immature Christian or even a non-Christian. Tozer makes a point:

> When reproved, pay no attention to the source. Do not ask whether it is a friend or an enemy that reproves you. An enemy is often of greater value to you than a friend because he is not influenced by sympathy.[47]

The life of Josiah is a warning to us all. Josiah was one of Israel's great kings and was instrumental in bringing revival, yet he lost his life because he did not think God would speak through his enemy, Neco, king of Egypt:

> *Josiah would not turn away from him...nor did he listen to the words of Neco from the mouth of God.*[48]

3. Take a genuine interest in other people.

> *Don't become snobbish, but take a real interest in ordinary people...*[49]

If you ever wonder why your friendships suffer, this may be a very good reason. A key to effective ministry is developing genuine interest in other people. Jesus seemed genuinely interested in people he met; He took them seriously and often started a conversation by asking them questions. Two good examples of this are His conversations with the Samaritan woman[50] and the father of the epileptic boy.[51]

I have met people who give me an immediate first impression that they could care less about me or that they were doing me a tremendous favor to be giving me their time. I have also met people who have made me feel, when talking with me, that I am very special to them. Scripture tells us to have the same attitude Jesus had and *not merely look out for your own personal interests, but also for the interests of others.*[52] If not careful, we can become so busy talking about <u>our</u> interests that we never ask about the other's interest: e.g.

-How do <u>you</u> feel about this?
-Tell me about <u>your</u> children...
-What has been going on with <u>your</u> work lately?

By taking a selfless interest in others, not only will we become more effective listeners, but we also might find ourselves with a few more friends!

4. Listen fully before you speak.

> *He who answers before listening -- that is his folly and shame.*[53]

Once a co-worker and I were discussing purchasing a small copying machine to be used for the church which would cost $1,500.00. A member of the church, overhearing our conversation, thought he heard us discussing a <u>coffee</u> machine! For several weeks after that, this brother went around shaking his head and wondering what kind of expensive coffee we were drinking! Finally we discussed it one day and the matter was resolved. I have learned in my limited experience of dealing with some severe marriage problems that it is essential in most cases to <u>hear both sides</u> before I make too many conclusions:

> *Any story sounds true until someone tells the other side and sets the record straight.*[54]

In becoming effective listeners, we must also learn to hear what is below the surface. Jesus said, *Take care* *<u>how</u>* *you listen...*[55] A person may be saying one thing with lips but deep inside be crying out something else; for example, "I have a headache!" may be an attempt to say, "Nobody is paying any attention to me."

Our Lord could minister so effectively because *He knew what was in a man.*[56] Since we do not know, we must depend upon the Holy Spirit to reveal to us the <u>real need</u>. Sometimes we jump to conclusions and give out quick, easy solutions to very complex problems. I have noticed some television preachers seem to limit all their answers to about fifty verses in the Bible while ignoring many other relevant passages. Watchman Nee illustrates an important point:

> The story is told of an elderly doctor whose entire stock of medicines consisted of two kinds -- castor oil and quinine. No matter what complaint his patients suffered from, he invariably doled out either the one medicine or the other. Many Christian workers treat those who come to them just like that. They have one or two pet subjects, and however varied the ailments of those who seek them out, they talk to them along their one or two special lines. Such workers cannot be of any real help because they can only talk; they cannot listen...[57]

Let us learn to be sensitive to the heart of a man, not just the outward words. If we have a listening ear, it will help us to care and minister effectively, like the Master we follow.

NOTES

1.I Kings 12:8,15

2.I Kings 11:9-13; 12:15

3.Ex. 15:26

4.Deut. 28:15 NAS mg.

5.James 1:19

6.Prov. 29:20 New English Bible

7.e.g. Matt. 11:15; 13:16

8.Is. 50:4 NAS

9.Prov. 18:2

10.Prov. 14:3 Good News Bible

11.Prov. 1:5

12.Paul Billheimer, Love Covers (Christian Literature Crusade, Ft. Washington, PA, 1981) p. 110-111

13.Watchman Nee, The Character of God's Workman (Christian Fellowship Publishers, NY, 1988) p.162

14.Psa. 81:13

15.Ex. 21:5-7

16.Lance Lambert, article "The Cross" in Christ, the Cross, the Church (Elim Publications, Hong Kong, 1990) p.124-125

17.Rev. 3:20

18.story told by DeVern Fromke, Life's Ultimate Privilege (Sure Foundation, Indianapolis, IN, 1986) Chapter 8

19.I Kings 19:11-12

20.Matt. 17:5

21.Matt. 15:6 KJV

22.II Kings 17:40

23.Josh. 9:14

24.Fromke, Life's Ultimate Privilege, Chapter 8, p.10

25.John 10:27 Wuest The New Testament: An Expanded Translation

26.Acts 16:14 Living Bible

27.I Sam. 3:10

28.Is. 28:23
29.Prov. 23:22
30.Eph. 6:2-3
31.Ex. 18:24
32.I Thes. 5:21
33.Matt. 27:19-20
34.I John 4:6
35.Lk. 10:16
36.Prov. 15:32 New English Bible
37.A.W. Tozer, The Root of the Righteous (Christian Publications, Harrisburg, PA)
38.Matt. 18:16-17
39.Acts 5:29
40.Deut. 17:12-13
41.Ecc. 4:13 NAS
42.Prov. 12:15 Living Bible
43.Prov. 12:1 Living Bible
44.Prov. 19:20 Living Bible
45.II Tim. 4:3
46.Lk. 2:46
47.Tozer, Ibid.
48.II Chron. 35:21-23
49.Rom. 12:16 Phillips
50.John 4
51.Mk. 9:16-29
52.Phil. 2:4-5
53.Prov. 18:13
54.Prov. 18:17 Living Bible
55.Luke 8:18
56.John 2:25
57.Watchman Nee, The Normal Christian Worker (Church Book Room, Hong Kong, 1965), p.47

Chapter Three

Responding in Meekness

Watchman Nee, the influential Chinese Bible teacher, once faced a major spiritual crisis. In the prime of his ministry in the 1940's, Nee was excommunicated by four other elders of the church in which he had faithfully served. Because of his over-involvement in a pharmaceutical company, which led to financial losses of some church members, Nee's integrity was called into question. Other issues were brought in, and Nee was asked to step down. For two years after this there is no evidence that the other elders made any approach to him. In the biography of his life, we see this godly man's response:

> For his part he [Nee] recalled Margaret Barber's meekness in the face of his own tirades and once again he made no attempt at self-vindication but accepted their action as a discipline from God who would in His own way justify Himself.
>
> Understandably Charity [his wife], who was actively helping him in the business, did not

> at once appreciate this attitude. One day she heard Watchman answer a phone call in which the voice at the other end went on and on at a high volume. Watchman simply listened to it all, answering now and again with "Yes...yes...thank you...thank you." "Whoever was that?" she asked, when he had rung off. "It was a brother telling me all I have been doing wrong." "And were you guilty of all that?" she asked. "No," he replied. "Then why did you not give him an explanation instead of just saying thank you?" she exclaimed impatiently. "If anyone exalts Watchman Nee to heaven," was the reply, "he is still Watchman Nee. And if anyone tramples him down to hell, he remains Watchman Nee." God was righteous, and to him that was sufficient. Characteristically he is known to have ministered secret financial help to some of the brothers who were opposing him.[1]

Over the years as I have observed and counseled couples with numerous marriage problems, I have noticed in almost every case of unresolved tensions the absence of one quality that, if it were present in one or both partners, would have made a major breakthrough in resolving their problem. The quality is meekness, which is vividly portrayed in our example above. True meekness reveals the very nature of Christ Himself and it is the one quality that distinguishes between saint and sinner. This character trait is imperative for any growing Christian; no matter how many years he has in the faith or how much knowledge he has of spiritual matters, his true testimony will be reflected in the way he responds or fails to respond in meekness. Scripture speaks of a *meek and quiet spirit, which is in the sight of God of great price.*[2] Andrew Murray emphasized the necessity of this attribute:

> "A meek spirit is of great price in God's sight; it is the choicest ornament of the Beloved Son."[3]

Jesus certainly placed a high priority on this quality:

> *Blessed are the meek, for they will inherit the earth.*[4]

Meekness is a Greek word rich in meaning; no single English word can translate it. The Greek word (*praus*) can mean "gentle," "pleasant," "mild," or "soothing."[5] The word describes the quiet and friendly composure which does not become embittered or angry at what is unpleasant, whether in the form of people or circumstances.[6] Aristotle used *praus* to describe the median between extremes of anger and indifference.[7] In other words, the meek person will always be angry at the right time and never angry at the wrong time. Meekness is not just a quiet voice or a gentle disposition; behind many a gentle voice is a stubborn spirit. Gentleness can be just a biological fact; e.g., some dogs are more gentle than other dogs. The meekness or gentleness believers should develop, however, is something God-produced; it is a fruit of the Holy Spirit.[8]

Praus is also used for a beast that has been tamed; a horse who once roamed wild, but now has come under the discipline of a bit and bridle. William Barclay explains further:

> Now herein lies the secret of the meaning of *praus*. There is gentleness in *praus* but behind the gentleness there is the strength of steel, for the supreme characteristic of the man who is *praus* is the man who is under perfect control. It is not a spineless gentleness, a sentimental fondness, a passive quietism. It is strength under control.[9]

How to Recognize a Meek Man

1. A meek man will know who he is in God; he will not feel inferior or superior.

Jesus describes Himself as *meek and lowly in heart*[10] and yet we do not get the impression He was a "weakling" or "pushover." Moses describes himself as *very meek, above all the men which were upon the face of the earth,*[11] and yet this man could act decisively and blaze with anger as the need arose. Jesus and Moses, in describing their meekness, could do so because they were neither proud nor self-demeaning; they were simply honest in their estimation of themselves. We are urged to do the same in Scripture, for this is true meekness.[12] A.W. Tozer remarks:

> The meek man is not a human mouse afflicted with a sense of his own inferiority...he has accepted God's estimate of his own life. He knows he is weak and helpless as God has declared him to be, but paradoxically, he knows at the same time that he is in the sight of God of more importance than angels. In himself nothing, in God, everything.[13]

2. The meek man will be a gentle man who is approachable.

I have known men who were spiritually gifted and quite knowledgeable of deep things of God, yet they disqualified themselves from ministry because they were not approachable. One such man, if confronted by young believers about a problem in his life, would become defensive and turn things around so that <u>they</u> went away feeling <u>they</u> were the ones with a problem!

Watchman Nee comments:

> There are several qualities which characterize a person who is meek. He is approachable -- so easy to have contact with, to talk to, and to make inquiry of...Open to the opinions of others, he welcomes instructions...[14]

Paul, in dealing with congregations was not a hard, "religious dictator" or "God's Answer Man" for their lives. He came with a gentle spirit:

> *What do you prefer? Shall I come to you with a whip, or in love and with a gentle spirit?*[15]

> *But we were gentle among you, like a mother caring for her little children.*[16]

Believers who are harsh and "cannot be crossed" will be of little use in the kingdom of God. If we are to be known for any attribute, may it be a gentle spirit; Scripture says, *Have a reputation for gentleness.*[17]

3. A meek man will not insist upon his rights.

Bill Gothard has defined meekness as "yielding my personal rights and expectations to God."[18] How many marriages would have been salvaged if both parties were equally willing to release their rights? Oswald Chambers says, "The only right a Christian has is the right to give up his rights."[19] God displayed true meekness in coming to earth as a human baby, born of a woman in a humble manger:

> *Jesus Christ...though he was God, did not demand and cling to his rights as God, but laid aside his mighty power and glory, taking the disguise of a slave and becoming like men...*[20]

We are encouraged to have this same attitude that Christ had.[21] Throughout the Bible we have numerous examples of those who were willing to relinquish their rights. Here are a few:

* **Abraham:** When Abraham's family became crowded in a parcel of land shared with his nephew Lot, their herdsmen began quarreling, and Abraham decided it would be best to split apart and settle in different regions. Lot took first pick and chose the best-looking land. Abraham, the elder of the two, could have easily insisted on first choice; he could have said, "Lot, you know I am the one whom God speaks to and I am the one He has chosen to father a great nation. Now step aside and let me choose..." No, Abraham deferred to his nephew but as a result ended up settling in God's chosen land.[22]

* **Isaac:** After Isaac's men dug a well (no easy task in those days) the herdsmen of Gerar claimed the well saying, *The well is ours!*[23] Isaac's men moved on and dug another well, but once again Gerar's men laid claim. A second time Isaac's men moved to another location. Surely this would have been a time to claim one's rights and legitimately fight! However, this meek response had a true testimony to Gerar and his men. They later came to make a treaty with Isaac and in their own words they said, *We saw clearly that the Lord was with you...you are blessed by the Lord.*[24]

* **David:** In the midst of David's reign, his son Absalom threatened to usurp his father's throne and divide the kingdom.

David, in a spirit of meekness, did nothing to retain his position, and he put his confidence in God:

> *And the king said,..."If I find favor in the sight of the Lord, then He will bring me back again..."*[25]

I realize some unstable souls may take these words to mean that women should be passive "doormats" or that child abuse should be permitted. These are other matters; our Lord is deeply concerned for our welfare, and sometimes practical steps need to be taken to insure one's safety. My remarks, however, are directed toward the "spirit of this age" which is increasingly absorbed with self and demanding one's rights. Unfortunately, too many Christians have also been affected. Tozer expressed his concern years ago:

> Few sights are more depressing than that of a professing Christian defending his or her supposed rights and bitterly resisting any attempt to violate them. Such a Christian has never accepted the way of the cross.[26]

The opposite of meekness is anger. There is a place for righteous anger, but most of our anger is selfish anger -- e.g., someone irritates me, or fails to appreciate me, or damages something that is mine. When we feel slighted we respond in one of these two ways -- anger or meekness. The first murder in the human race took place because of selfish anger; Cain was upset because his offering was not accepted as was Abel's:

> *Then the Lord said to Cain, "Why are you angry? Why is your face downcast? If you do what is right, will you not be accepted? But if you do not do what is right, sin is crouching at your door; it desires to*

have you, but you must master it."[27]

If we become angry as we insist on getting our "fair share" or "what is rightfully mine," we not only are failing to respond in the spirit of meekness, but we are opening the door for evil influences. One translation in the above passage says, *But if you refuse to obey, watch out. Sin is waiting to attack you, longing to destroy you.*[28] Another version says, *Sin is like a demon crouching at the door. It shall be eager for you, and you will be mastered by it.*[29] We will do well in the majority of situations if we respond as Jesus would -- in meekness.

4. A meek man will be forbearing.

> *With all humility and gentleness, with patience, showing forbearance to one another in love...*[30]

To forbear our brethren is to show a gentle and patient attitude toward folks we normally would have little to do with. Literally "forbear" means "to put up with."[31] The Amplified Bible in the above verse says, *bearing with one another and making allowances because you love one another.*[32] God will often send folks into our churches who need a lot of help --obnoxious personalities, unseemly table manners, goofy humor, or even unattractive physical qualities. Our natural tendency will be to flee, but God has called us to love. Even among Christians whom we deeply respect, as we become better acquainted, we may begin to notice some peculiarities, certain qualities which seem to be entirely out of place.

If we fail to show forbearance, it limits our ministry to others and produces turmoil within us. We will especially be tested when we are slandered or falsely accused. Everything in our flesh will rise up and want to defend self, but the Spirit of Christ will nudge us in another direction:

> *To this you were called, because Christ suffered for you, leaving you an example, that you should follow in his steps. "He committed no sin, and no deceit was found in his mouth." When they hurled their insults at him, he did not retaliate; when he suffered, he made no threats. Instead, he entrusted himself to him who judges justly.*[33]

An example of this spirit of meekness is found in the life of the eighteenth century English evangelist, George Whitefield. At one point in his ministry, Whitefield received a vicious letter accusing him of wrongdoing. His reply was brief and courteous: "I thank you heartily for your letter. As for what you and my other enemies are saying against me, I know worse things about myself than you will ever say about me. With love in Christ, George Whitefield."[34] He did not try to defend himself, but entrusted himself to the Righteous Judge.

Jonathan Edwards, the renowned theologian and contemporary of Whitefield, encouraged this same spirit:

> If you are not disposed to bear injuries meekly, then you are not equipped to live in this evil world. We do not dwell in a world of purity, innocence and love, but one that is fallen, corrupt, miserable and wicked...Therefore, if you do not have a spirit of meekness, calmness, and long-suffering to bear offenses in such a world, then you will be miserable indeed.
>
> If every injury and reproach, every malicious and unjust deed ruffles your spirit, then you are in perpetual turmoil. Even unintentional remarks or deeds by your brothers in the Lord will disturb you if you are not dependent on the gentle, long-suffering of the Spirit of God.[35]

Patience With All Men

In Christian service we must be prepared to deal with a variety of people in a variety of situations. Some will need a lot of grace; some will need a firm hand. All will need our patience:

> *And we urge you, brothers, warn those who are idle, encourage the timid, help the weak, be patient with everyone.*[36]

We need to show the same patience to others that our Lord shows to us.[37] Our long-suffering Lord Jesus has *unlimited patience*[38] with us and therefore, anytime we feel our patience wearing thin, let us stop and think how patient He has been with us! It was His forbearance, patience, and incredible kindness that saved us in the first place.[39] If we are lacking in patience, God will grant it to those who desire it and who are willing not to invariably run from unpleasant situations and/or people.

Patience is essential for all who serve the Lord, and especially for those who are leaders. Without patience a man will seldom be a leader in the Lord's church, regardless of his preaching and administrative gifts. Charles Swindoll comments:

> If one attempts to lead a congregation without this Spirit-given virtue [patience], he is driven to frustration, irritability, and severity. His pulpit becomes an avenue of anger, his preaching a diatribe of demands, and his person insulting and intolerant as Diotrophes of old.[40]

There are three types of people we need to especially be patient with, showing all manner of meekness. The first category is **those who have been caught in sin:**

> *Brethren, even if a man is caught in any trespass, you who are spiritual, restore such a one in a spirit of gentleness; looking to yourselves, lest you too be tempted.*[41]

Volumes could be written of the innumerable believers who have slipped into sin and subsequently been harshly rejected by a church group with no love and no meekness. Sin needs to be dealt with, but only with a meek and patient spirit. The word "restore" in the above verse is the Greek word for "repair" or "mend", used in one gospel account of fishermen mending broken nets.[42] Even if church discipline needs to be enforced upon those who are unrepentant and stubborn concerning ongoing sin, it must be done in meekness with restoration the goal.

A second group that requires our patience is **those mixed-up concerning the truth:**

> *God's people must not be quarrelsome; they must be gentle, patient teachers of those who are wrong. Be humble when you are trying to teach those who are mixed-up concerning the truth. For if you talk meekly and courteously to them they are more likely, with God's help, to turn away from their wrong ideas and believe what is true.*[43]

The best example of this patience is seen in the way Aquila and his wife, Priscilla, dealt with Apollos, a young man who was teaching about Jesus. Apollos' was a *learned man...with great fervor,* but his knowledge about Jesus was limited.[44] Instead of being critical or having "preacher stew" for lunch, Aquila and Priscilla invited this young man into their home and *explained to him the way of God more adequately.*[45] Without the time and support of this couple, Apollos may never have become as effective and widespread in his preaching as he eventually did. Sometimes those who are limited in knowledge or even confused concerning the truth will respond to someone who takes a personal interest in them, patiently teaching them the word more adequately.

A third category of believers to whom we especially need to respond in meekness is **those who are weak in faith:**

> *Accept him whose faith is weak, without passing judgment on disputable matters...*
> *Accept one another, then, just as Christ accepted you, in order to bring praise to God.*[46]

These believers who are "weak" are those without strength, power or ability. They will be those who stumble frequently, who do not seem to "have it all together," and who often have little natural personal appeal. Sometimes the weak in the faith can be a lot of trouble as they tend to become picky (and sometimes peculiar) over non-essential matters. We are reminded in the above verse to accept such a one in exactly the same manner Christ accepted us. Being kind, patient, and forbearing to weaker brethren is not easy, but it is a mark of true Christ-like character.

> *We who are strong ought to bear with the failings of the weak and not to please ourselves. Each of us should please his neighbor for his good, to build him up.*[47]

A major mark of spiritual strength is how well we bear (put up with) the shortcomings of weak believers. This calls for a denial of self; another version of the above verse says, *we should not just go our own sweet way...For even Christ did not choose his own pleasure.*[48]

In attempting to become the Lord's "glorious church" [i.e., a church which is wholehearted about seeking God's truth], I know some groups who only concentrate on becoming "the overcomers" [i.e., those who are strong and mighty in faith], and no allowance is made for weaker brethren. The elimination of the weak, however, is the death of fellowship. Dietrich Bonhoeffer once said:

> The exclusion of the weak and insignificant, the seemingly useless people, from a Christian community may actually mean the exclusion of Christ; in the poor brother Christ is knocking at the door. We must, therefore, be very careful at this point.[49]

This job of caring for the weak is not the job of a few pastors or "special saints;" it is the duty of every believer: *And we urge you, brothers...help the weak,be patient with everyone.*[50]

Let us major in meekness, being patient and forbearing with all men. If we learn to respond in this spirit, one thing we can be assured of -- the Lord's favor and presence will be upon us: *Let your forbearing spirit be known to all men. The Lord is near!*[51]

NOTES

1.Angus I. Kinnear, Against the Tide (Christian Literature Crusade, Ft. Washington, PA) p.127

2.I Pet. 3:4 KJV

3.Andrew Murray, The Believer's Secret of Living Like Christ (Bethany House Publishers, Minneapolis, MN, 1985) p.134

4.Matt. 5:5

5.Gerhard Friedrich, Theological Dictionary of the New Testament, Vol. 6 (Eerdmans, Grand Rapids, MI, 1968) p.645

6.IBID., p.645

7.IBID.,p.646

8.Gal. 5:23 KJV

9.William Barclay, New Testament Words (SCM Press, London, 1964) p.241

10.Matt. 11:29 KJV

11.Num. 12:3 KJV

12.Rom. 12:3

13.A.W. Tozer, Renewed Day by Day (Fleming Revell, Old Tappan, NJ) Sept. 14 devotional

14.Watchman Nee, The Release of the Spirit (Sure Foundation, Indianapolis, IN, 1965) p.85

15.I Cor. 4:21

16.I Thes. 2:7

17.Phil 4:5 Phillips

18.from Bill Gothard's "Character Clues", Box One, Oak Brook, IL.

19.Harry Verploegh, Oswald Chambers: The Best From All His Books (Thomas Nelson, Nashville, TN, 1987) p.294

20.Phil 2:6-7 Living Bible

21.Phil 2:5

22.Genesis 13

23.Gen. 26:20

24.Gen. 26:19-29

25.II Sam. 15:25

26.A.W.Tozer, Of God and Men (Christian Publications, Harrisburg, PA, 1960) p.89

27.Gen. 4:6-7

28.Gen. 4:7 Living Bible

29.Gen. 4:7 New English Bible

30.Eph. 4:2 NAS

31.Same Greek word is also used in Mk. 9:19

32.Eph. 4:2 Amplified Bible

33.I Pet. 2:21-23

34.Our Daily Bread (Grand Rapids, MI) Aug. 92

35.Jonathan Edwards and Andrew Murray, The Believer's Secret of Christian Love (Bethany House, Minneapolis, MN 1990) p.55

36.I Thes. 5:14

37.Matt. 18:29,33

38.I Tim 1:16

39.Rom. 2:4 see NAS

40.Charles Swindoll, Growing Strong in the Seasons of Life (Multnomah Press, Portland, OR, 1983) p.237

41.Gal. 6:2 NAS

42.Greek "katartizo" also used in Matt. 4:21

43.II Tim. 2:24-25 Living Bible

44.Acts 18:24-25

45.Acts 18:26

46.Rom. 14:1;15:7

47.Rom. 15:1-2

48.Rom. 15:1-2 Phillips

49.Dietrich Bonhoeffer, Life Together (SCM Press, London, 1949) p.28

50.I Thes. 5:14

51.Phil 4:5 NAS

Chapter Four

Bearing Our Cross Daily

For the message of the cross is foolishness to those who are perishing, but to us who are being saved it is the power of God....
When I came to you, brothers, I did not come with eloquence or superior wisdom as I proclaimed to you the testimony about God. For I resolved to know nothing while I was with you except Jesus Christ and him crucified.[1]

Throughout the pages of Christian history the cross of Jesus Christ has recurrently been a neglected subject. This is not to say the cross has been hidden from view; indeed, it is the frequent theme in many church hymns in just about any denomination across this land. Probably the most popular symbol from church buildings is that of the cross. Many enjoy wearing a cross around their necks, and sometimes feel more secure because of it. We could visit any town in America and soon see the symbol of the cross. In our own state someone has erected hundreds of steel crosses, planted in groups of three, in many conspicuous places along interstate highways.

Many believers only have a limited knowledge of the cross; mostly from preaching about the benefits of Jesus' death on the cross for us, i.e., the forgiveness of sins, the defeat of Satan, and the assurance of life forever. These truths should never be diminished in value; the very center of the gospel message revolves around the all-important fact *that Christ died for our sins and rose again according to Scripture.*[2]

There is something, however, that is still missing...

The Cross For Me...The Cross In Me

There is a twofold cross for every believer: the cross for me and the cross in me. In other words, we not only have an outward cross, but also an inward cross. The outward cross deals with sin; the inward cross deals with self. More than any New Testament writer, the apostle Paul seemed to know experientially the reality of the twofold cross:

> *For we know that our old self was crucified with him so that the body of sin might be done away with, that we should no longer be slaves to sin.*[3]
>
> *I have been crucified with Christ and I no longer live, but Christ lives in me. The life I live in the body, I live by faith in the Son of God, who loved me and gave himself for me.*[4]

Not only was Christ crucified on the cross, but we were crucified with Him. This is not just a theological fact; it is a practical reality that identifies those who really belong to Christ.

Paul said, *Those who belong to Christ Jesus have crucified the sinful nature with its passions and desires.*[5] Notice concerning "those who belong to Jesus," Scripture doesn't mention having the right church membership or believing the right church doctrine, it simply draws attention to our identification with Jesus' crucifixion. What many Bible teachers call "the crucified life" is no option; it is the true test of our profession of Christianity. On a daily basis we are called to identify with the cross of Jesus and take up our own cross:

> *Then he said to them all: "If anyone would come after me, he must deny himself and take up his cross daily and follow me."*[6]

A cross is not just "a very beautiful thing." In Jesus' time the cross was the most despised and disgusting emblem in the Roman empire; no Roman citizen was killed on a cross, only the worst criminals. It was the common method of executing slaves and a most horrifying method of death. In his classic book on the cross, Born Crucfied, L. E. Maxwell says,

> The Roman orator, Cicero, summarized the attitude of the ancient world to the cross when he said: "Not only let the cross be absent from the person of Roman citizens, but its very name from their thoughts, eyes and ears." Two thousand years ago we find no halo of glory, no beautiful associations of history, no nobility, and no thought of heroic sacrifice attached to the cross.[7]

For the believer, taking up his cross is no enjoyable matter nor is it something he would naturally want to do. After all, who wants to "die"?

What It Means To Take Up One's Cross?

There are many misconceptions about what it means to "bear one's cross." A "cross" is not a physical ailment -e.g., migraine headaches, arthritis, or rheumatism. A "cross" we bear is not an unreasonable wife or a lazy husband. A "cross" is not an unpleasant environment one has to work in that includes cursing, harassment, and lack of appreciation. All these experiences may be burdens or inescapable limitations, but they are not crosses.

The following may give a better idea what a cross means:

1. To take up one's cross means to lose one's life.

> *Anyone who does not take his cross and follow me is not worthy of me. Whoever finds his life will lose it, and whoever loses his life for my sake will find it.*[8]

The above verse is Jesus' most frequently quoted statement. It appears six times in the New Testament and is in every gospel. To "lose one's life" does not mean being heroic and jumping in front of a car which is about to crush a young child. The Greek word for "life" is "psuche", from which we get the English "psyche." This is the realm of the soul - the mind, will, and emotions, i.e., what I think, what I want, and what I feel. When we deny ourselves, this does not mean we are to deny ourselves things; it means I say no to myself! Self-denial [of things] can still be self-centered, especially if we feel proud about what we have accomplished. Denial of self, on the other hand, is Christ-centered as it focuses our attention away from ourselves to Him.

Jesus not only deals with our sin nature and acts of sin, He also deals with our legitimate self as well. Martyn Lloyd Jones has said the true test of whether someone is teaching the cross rightly or wrongly is whether or not it is an offence to the natural man.[9] Scripture mentions *the offense of the cross.*[10] Many movements today encourage us to realize ourselves, express ourselves, indulge ourselves, or better ourselves. These are all contrary to Jesus' simple words: *deny yourself.*

The inward cross will deal with self-love at its very root, in the very depths of our being where we can hardly detect it. It means we are willing to lay down the things our self values the most -- our opinions, our ambitions, our desires, and our hopes. It means I am willing to give it all up that Christ may have His way in me. A real cross in our lives involves the will; it is more than just saying "no" to things, it means saying "yes" to something for Jesus' sake.

The bearing of our cross is not a dismal thing in the end; its end result is <u>life</u>:

> *I tell you the truth, unless a kernel of wheat falls to the ground and dies, it remains only a single seed. But if it dies, it produces many seeds.*[11]

Our fleshly nature does not like the way of the cross, but it is the only pathway to fruitfulness. The above verse was modeled in John the Baptist. John had been the forerunner for Jesus, announcing to great crowds that the Messiah would soon appear. When Jesus came on the scene, John said, "*He must increase, but I must decrease.*"[12] John was willing to take a step back that the people might see Jesus. This is the real test of whether or not the cross is operating in our lives: what do people see in us? Are they impressed with us or with Christ in us? What do we want people to see in us -- ourselves looking good or simply Christ?

2. To take up one's cross means to take the hard way to glory.

> *For the gate is narrow and the way is hard, that leads to life, and those who find it are few.*[13]

From childhood Jesus knew that he was headed for the greatest victory, the most powerful conquest this universe has ever seen. Jesus also knew, however, it would not be an easy road to walk.

Humans normally prefer the easy way. This is apparent in our national school system and work ethic. Major corporations have tremendous difficulty in hiring young people to take ordinary responsibilities and work their way "up the ladder." Kids today want the "easy way to success" and neglect the Biblical work ethic:

> *Steady plodding brings prosperity, hasty speculation brings poverty...*
> *He who works his land will have abundant food, but the one who chases fantasies will have his fill of poverty. A faithful man will be richly blessed, but one eager to get rich will not go unpunished.*[14]

In Jesus' three temptations which preceded His ministry, one of the Devil's tests was to tell Jesus a quick method to build a following: "Jesus, go up to that tallest building in Jerusalem and throw yourself down. The angels will catch you --after all, God has promised their protection." What was the nature of this temptation? In this subtle suggestion Satan was offering Jesus <u>the easy way</u>. Jesus, however, knew what the Father expected and would not shrink back from the life he would live out and the cup of suffering of which he would need to partake in order for mankind to be saved. Jesus took the hard road to glory, and we must follow in His footsteps.

To go the Lord's way will not always be the popular way, but it will be the right way. Multitudes of high school and college-age students learn to bear a cross when they decide to follow Christ rather than follow peer pressure. A Christian businessman bears a cross when he forfeits dishonest money by making honest decisions, all of which seem absurd in the eyes of his business associates. The way of the cross, for any who dare to bear it, is not an easy way.

3. To take up one's cross is to daily demonstrate Christ's life in you.

Our cross will become very practical; it is a daily principal which can affect even the smallest details of our lives. A true test of a genuine believer is that *he must deny himself and take up his cross daily...*[15] God will give us frequent opportunities where we must choose to express either the self-life (the old nature) or the Christ-life (the new nature). We will fail at times, but God has lifelong "schooling" in transforming our lives to be more like His son.[16]

Someone has said that the cross is "where God's will crosses your will." That is a good definition! Watchman Nee says the cross is "the will of God joyfully accepted."[17]
This gets very practical:

e.g., Men, you want to go hunting, but you sense your family needs you at home...
e.g., Your favorite television program has just started, but you notice out the window that your elderly neighbor needs some help...
e.g., You are standing in a long line and someone butts in front of you...

When we deny ourselves what is often even a legitimate right (after all, don't men have a right to go hunting?), the spirit of Christ can be manifest through us. When a dying to self-interests takes place, the life of Christ is displayed to others:

> *For we who are alive are always being given over to death for Jesus' sake, so that his life may be revealed in our mortal body. So then, death is at work in us, but life is at work in you.*[18]

The cross can often be applied in personal relationships. How do we respond when we have been offended, hurt, or misunderstood? Do we react in the flesh or act in the spirit of Christ? If husbands and wives learned to take up the cross, it would eliminate 95% of their marital problems. What happens when we are taken advantage of (e.g., in a business transaction)? Do we rant and rave like those who do not know Christ? Or do we act like godly men of old who *joyfully accepted the confiscation of their property.*[19] This is not to say that we never pursue legitimate channels of the law; what we are emphasizing here is the right spirit. If a man does not have the spirit (nature) of Christ, Scripture says *he does not belong to Christ.*[20] This kind of attitude is demonstrated when someone wants to sue us and take our overcoat; we give him our shirt as well. If someone puts us to inconvenience and asks us to go a mile, we go two miles![21] This kind of response is not natural; it must be Christ in us responding.

When We Can Tell The Cross Is Not Operating In Our Lives

Just before Jesus died, a passer-by insulted the Son of God by saying, "*Save yourself! Come down from the cross!*"[22]

This is a possibility we also face on a regular basis. We can choose at any given time to go the way of self and "come down" from the cross. Paul Billheimer, in Destined for the Cross, explains the necessity of making the right choice:

> Right here is the secret of victory: not a past crisis primarily, but a present, day-by-day yielding to the cross. There is only one place of power over Satan and that is the cross. It was on the cross and by the cross that Christ overcame him. The cross was his undoing. And that is the only place where Satan is ever defeated. The only time that Satan cannot touch us is when we are upon the cross....If you look back on your own life, the only time you have been defeated was when you came down from the cross.[23]

Although it is no exhaustive list, the following are seven indicators of when the cross principle is not operating in our lives:[24]

1. The cross is not operating when we are easily offended and worry about "fair treatment."

If we are frequently touchy, irritable, and "getting our feathers ruffled," it is a sure indicator we are not bearing our cross. Also, if we constantly excuse ourselves, defend ourselves, and vindicate ourselves, it is another indicator. Tozer says,

> Christians who understand the true meaning of the cross will never whine about being treated unfairly. Whether or not they are given fair treatment will never enter their heads. They know they have been called to follow Christ, and

> certainly Christ did not receive anything remotely approaching fair treatment from mankind.[25]

2. The cross is not operating when we are self-centered (even in our spiritual affairs).

William Law, the seventeenth-century English devotional writer, comments:

> Self is the root, the tree, and the branches of all the evils of our fallen state. We are without God, because we are in the life of self. Self-love, self-esteem, and self-seeking are the very essence and life of pride; and the devil, the first father of pride, is never absent from them, nor without power in them.[26]

In writing to Timothy, the apostle Paul described the end of time: *In the last days difficult times will set in, for men will live a life that is centered in self......*[27] We are truly seeing this in our generation. Few of us can fathom just how much self-centeredness there is in us, even though we are Christians. Derek Prince, one who has taught and ministered to thousands of believers during the past fifty years, shares his observation:

> Self-centeredness has been one of the most obvious effects of the devil's influence in a human life. In ministering deliverance to those afflicted by evil spirits, I have observed that such people are nearly always intensely self-centered. They delight to sit and talk for hours in counseling sessions and to expatiate in wearisome detail on all their problems. They fail to realize that the more they talk about themselves, the

stronger they make the bars of their own prison.[28]

3. The cross is not operating when we become stubborn (stiff-necked).

> *A man who remains stiff-necked after many rebukes will suddenly be destroyed--without remedy.*[29]

Roy Hession is the author of an exceptional book about the cross, Calvary Road. In his autobiography, Hession shares a particular experience which brought him to better appreciate "the crucified life" and inspire the soon writing of his book. At a Bible conference, he was deeply touched by a motto card:

Lord, bend that proud and stiff-necked "I",
   Help me to bow the neck and die,
Beholding Him on Calvary,
   Who bowed His head for me.

In his own words, Hession describes how he was pierced to the heart after reading the above words:

> I saw I was the proud, stiff-necked, unyielding man pictured in the letter "I", so quick to justify himself and to resent others. More moving to me was to see that same man on his knees, with his head bowed and face buried in his hands. He had seen Jesus and, ashamed, had taken the sinner's place and given up his rights to Him. I was immediately convicted that I had not been taking that place, nor had I been willing to bow the head and die to self. It was natural for me to stand up for myself. Little wonder that Jesus had not been able to live out His life in me and through me in all its sweetness and fullness. But I saw, too, in those days a new value in His blood which "makes the wounded whole."[30]

4. The cross is not operating when we are continually wounded in our self-esteem.

In 1986 George Gallup Jr. said his latest poll showed that one-third of Americans suffer from low self-esteem. He considered this to be the chief psychological malady of our day. People "without proper self-esteem" seem to always be getting down on themselves, looking inward, and dwelling on how people have mistreated or misunderstood them. Even though numerous contemporary Christian books emphasizes the need of self-esteem, this emphasis is absent in the Bible. In the apostolic writings, we see Christians urged to love God and love their brethren. No excuses are allowed and no circumstances considered. If we studied the culture of early Christianity, we would realize that family life was far from ideal and that many folks, if not most, grew up in environments that did not foster love and acceptance. The converted pagans in Corinth and other wicked cities were simply instructed to *pursue love.*[31]

Today some would say that a new believer cannot love others until he has proper self-esteem or is "healed in his damaged emotions." While some may need time to be restored and encouraged emotionally, we should be careful about placing unbiblical limits concerning God's commandments to love others.

5. The cross is not operating when we are reluctant to serve the Lord.

When we become absorbed with our self-interests and personal problems, we will usually be ineffective in serving the Lord. I remember a godly professor from college days who, despite his own share of problems, was a true servant of the Lord. He used to say, "In a sense, we are all spiritual cripples. Either we can spend our entire life dwelling on our <u>own</u> problems, or we can focus our energies on the problems of <u>others</u>, who may be needier than ourselves." I have never forgotten this word of wisdom.

6. The cross is not operating when we become fond of comfort.

One characteristic of the flesh [old nature] is that it will avoid anything that brings discomfort. God, however, is like a mother eagle that stirs up her nest;[32] He just doesn't let us get very comfortable for long. Stuart Briscoe once said, "God is not a recreational director on a cruise ship whose job is to give everyone a good time with no expense spared." The cross we carry is not a smooth and polished piece of wood; it is the "old rugged cross" -- it bruises the shoulders and leaves splinters in the fingers.

7. The cross is not operating when we become legalistic and harsh.

The legalist will emphasize all the "do's and don'ts" and will become upset at believers who do not follow rigid commandments as he tries to do. The legalist has missed the grace of God and finds it easier to walk in a highly regimented system than to daily walk in dependence of God. The work of the cross, on the other hand, will make us compassionate, considerate, and full of mercy.

In closing this chapter, let us consider this challenge by Thomas a' Kempis:

Why Not Take Up The Cross?

> Why, then, do you fear to take up the cross which fits you for the kingdom? In the cross there is life, in the cross is salvation; the cross defends against all enemies; in the cross there is the infusion of heavenly sweetness; in the cross is strength of mind, joy of spirit; the cross is the height of virtue and the perfection of sanctity. There is no happiness for the soul but in the cross. Take up, therefore, your cross and follow Jesus, and you shall live forever.[33]

NOTES

1.I Cor. 1:18; 2:1-2

2.I Cor. 15:3-4

3.Rom. 6:5-6

4.Gal. 2:20

5.Gal. 5:24

6.Lk. 9:23

7.L.E. Maxwell, Born Crucified (Moody Press, Chicago, 1945) p.31

8.Matt. 10:38-39

9.Martyn Lloyd-Jones, The Cross (Crossway Books, Westchester, IL, 1986) p. 45

10.Gal. 5:11

11.John 12:24

12.John 3:30 NAS

13.Matt. 7:14 RSV

14.Prov. 21:5 Liv. Bib.; Prov. 28:19-20 NIV

15.Luke 9:23

16.II Cor. 3:18

17.Watchman Nee, Twelve Baskets Full, Vol. 1 (Christian Literature Crusade, Ft. Washington, PA, 1965) p.94

18.II Cor. 4:11-12

19.Heb. 10:34

20.Rom. 8:9

21.Matt. 5:40-41

22.Matt. 27:40

23.Paul Billheimer, Destined for the Cross (Tyndale House, Wheaton, IL, 1983) p.20

24.Several of these indicators were shared on an excellent tape by Bob Mumford entitled "The Double Cross." c/o Life Changers, P.O. Box 98088, Raleigh, NC 27624

25.A.W. Tozer, This World: Playground or Battleground (Christian Publications, Camp Hill, PA, 1989) p.79

26.William Law, The Power of the Spirit (Bethany House Publishers, Minneapolis, MN, 1896) p.84

27.II Tim. 3:1-2 William Barclay's translation

28.Derek Prince, God is a Matchmaker (Chosen Books, Old Tappan, NJ, 1986) p.62

29.Prov. 29:1

30.Roy Hession, My Calvary Road (Zondervan, Grand Rapids, MI, 1978) p.90

31.I Cor. 14:1

32.Deut. 32:11

33.Thomas a' Kempis, Of the Imitation of Christ, p.11-12

Chapter Five

Ordering Our Lives Before The Lord

So Jotham became mighty because he ordered his ways before the Lord his God.[1]

When God created the universe, it was no haphazardly accomplished task; God is a God of order.[2] We can look at the mighty stars or a tiny butterfly and see the handiwork of a Creator God who desires for *all things to be done properly [beautifully and gracefully] and in an orderly manner [according to proper arrangement].*[3] The word orderly can be defined with many synonyms: "neat," "tidy," "shipshape," "well-regulated," and "arranged properly." The opposite word, disorderly, also has several synonyms: "confused," "irregular," "tangled," "disorganized," "complex," "gnarled," and "snarled." Which of these two words do we want to describe our lives?

Before going any further, let me emphasize that we can certainly go through life being very disorganized and haphazard and still experience the blessing of God on our lives. God's grace is certainly not restricted to how neat and orderly we are! It is my persuasion, however, that God can accomplish <u>much more</u> through our finite lives if they are in good order. In writing to the Colossian church, Paul said he rejoiced in seeing two qualities in their lives:

> *For though I am absent in body, yet I am with you in spirit, rejoicing to see your good order and the firmness of your faith in Christ.*[4]

The word *order* in the above verse is a military word which means "a good arrangement, an orderly condition."[5] If our lives are in "orderly condition," not only will we probably be more useful to the Lord, but also life will likely be more enjoyable.

Indicators of a Disorderly Life[6]

There are several obvious factors which reveal the disorganization in one's life. It is amazing how we can become accustomed to "life-as-it-is" and fail to notice things that are quite apparent to many other people. The following will usually reveal how disorderly we are:

* **Our car:** Is it dirty inside and out? Have we waxed it the past year? Have we <u>ever</u> waxed it?! Do we forget annual stickers and inspection? Do we have a record of maintenance or just wait until something goes wrong?

* **Our desk:** We can learn a lot about a person by looking at his/her desk. This is not to say that the desk of a businessman

or an active person should be bare; Scripture says, *An empty stable stays clean, but there is no income from an empty stable!*[7] When I was in retail business some years ago, if I ever had a completely clean desk, it was usually an indication business was slow! There is a difference, however, in a "well-used" desk top and a "cluttered" desk top. A cluttered desk will have litter, unanswered memos, and too many projects with which we are procrastinating.

* **A multitude of unfinished tasks:** We can know we are disorderly if we regularly forget appointments, fail to respond to telephone messages, and miss deadlines.

* **Little time for God:** Disorderly Christians often fail to enjoy intimacy with God as Bible reading becomes haphazard and prayer usually occurs "on the go."

How To Order Our Lives In Christ

We cannot overstress the fact that true order in our lives is only possible through a personal, vital relationship with Jesus Christ. In Christ *all things become new*[8] and this certainly includes what we do with our time. Billy Graham recently stated:

> The greatest waste in all the earth, which cannot be reclaimed, is our waste of the time God has given us each day.[9]

The lordship of Jesus should affect our priorities in life and even the way we use "our" leisure time. The following are very practical guidelines, and at least one of these should be applicable to every reader:

1. Do not let urgent demands on your life crowd out your top two priorities.

Jesus summed up all the Old Testament commandments in two simple instructions: first, we should love the Lord with all our heart, soul, strength, and mind; and second, love our neighbor as ourself.[10] Therefore, we could list our top two priorities in life as follows:

A. Time with God
B. Time with people
   1. our mate
   2. our children
   3. other believers (Gal. 6:10)
   4. non-believers

If we are lacking time for either of the above two categories, it is likely a sign that our priorities are mixed up. It is no easy task to use our time wisely in keeping priorities right, but God has provided all the time we need: 24 hours or 1,440 minutes a day. We have the exact same time in our day that the President of our country has and the exact same time that Billy Graham has. We do <u>not</u> need an extra six hours a day; we simply need to make better use of that which God has given.

We need to take time for intimate fellowship with God. This does not mean "praying on the run." The Scripture says that if we seek first the kingdom of God, the other things we need will be added.[11] C.S. Lewis said it this way: "Aim at heaven and you will get earth thrown in. Aim at earth and you will get neither." Martin Luther once said, "I have so much business I cannot get along without spending three hours daily in prayer." While most of us probably cannot spend three hours in prayer daily, there is a principle here. We have no good excuses for not spending <u>some</u> unhurried time with God every day.

People should be our second priority. Many believers get involved in numerous good activities, but do not seem to have time to spend on others. Jesus usually seemed to have time for people, and he was not so busy attending religious meetings that he had no time for sinners. Some believers focus so much on their own family ("us four and no more!") that there is little time for fellowship with other believers or friendship evangelism with non-Christians.

2. Make every minute count.

> *Live life, then, with a due sense of responsibility, not as men who do not know the meaning of life, but as those who do. Make the best use of your time, despite all the evils of these days.*[12]

It is not the supremely busy men who have no time. People who complain the most about all they have to do often actually have very little to do. Consider the following:

* Mary Slessor, famous missionary in Nigeria, later known as "The White Queen," began working at the age of eleven in a factory in Dundee from six in the morning to six at night. Despite her working hard and living in the home of a drunken father, she took time to educate herself for her future work.

* David Livingston began working in a cotton mill in Dumbarton when he was ten years old. Working from six in the morning to eight at night, he surely could have had an excuse not to study! Yet he so used his "leisure" hours that he mastered Latin and could read Horace and Virgil with ease before he was sixteen. By the time he was twenty-seven, he had worked his way through a medical course, as well as a course in

theology.[13]

* Ken Taylor, author of The Living Bible, in the midst of a full-time job, took time on the commuter ride between Wheaton and Chicago to translate the Scripture into language his children would understand. In the evenings he would check the original languages and "polish" his work. The result is a paraphrased version which has a distribution in excess of 25 million copies.

It is amazing what can be accomplished in just ten minutes. By reading just ten minutes an evening, an average reader can read a book within three to four weeks. That may not seem much, but ten minutes a day can average out to ten books a year. That's redeeming the time. We may not have extra hours in a day, but we all have extra minutes we can take advantage of. Charles Spurgeon gave the following illustration:

> Select a large box, and place in it as many cannon balls as it will hold, and it is, after a fashion full; but it will hold more if smaller matters can be found. Bring a quantity of marbles; very many of these may be packed in the spaces between the larger globes. The box is full now, but still only in a sense; it will contain more yet. There are spaces in abundance, into which you may shake a considerable quantity of small shot, and now the chest is filled beyond question; but yet there is room. You cannot put in another shot or marble, much less another ball, but you will find that several pounds of sand will slide down between the larger materials; and, even then between the granules of sand, if you empty yonder jug, there will be space for all the water, and for the same quantity several time

> repeated. Where there is no space for the great, there may be room for the little; where the little cannot enter, the less can make its way; and where the less is shut out, the least of all may find ample room. So where time is, as we say, fully occupied, there must be stray moments, occasional intervals, and bits of time which might hold a vast amount of usefulness in the course of months and years.[14]

The fact is -- we all find time to do what we really want to do. A young man may say he is much too busy in his job to serve the Lord, and yet one day he meets an attractive young lady and, guess what? He suddenly finds some extra time! A lot of time usage simply comes down to right priorities. I know of families who have chosen to live in modest homes and purchase used cars so the wife can be at home more and serve her children and other people. This is commendable. In a survey conducted for the Massachusetts Mutual Life Insurance Company, 35% of the parents polled said "time constraints" were the reason for declining family values. Yet 67% in the very same poll said they would accept a job that required more time away from home if it offered higher income or greater prestige.[15]

God has given us all the time we need -- for worship, work, family life, rest, and recreation. Balancing our time between these is not easy, but if we do not have time for the things we feel are really important, then one of two things is true: (1) we are doing something God does not want us to do, or (2) we are not doing it God's way. The trouble is not with God; it's with us!

Mark Porter encourages us to follow the example of Jesus, whose desire for us is not to make us "time nuts," but to accomplish all that the Father wants us to do -- with peace:

> At the end of three-and-a-half years of ministry, Jesus reported to His Father, "I have finished the work which thou gavest Me to do" (John 17:4 KJV). He accomplished more in that short span than anyone has accomplished in a lifetime, yet we never see Him in a frenzy to get things done. Nor was He too busy for others. Yet He was in control of His time and His life. He had a peace and a calmness which is not suggested in most time-management books. He wants us to have this too: "Peace I leave with you, My peace I give unto you" (John 14:27 KJV).[16]

3. Watch out for "time bandits."

If we stop and think about it, we will discover there is not just one major factor, but usually several little things that prevent us from an ordered life. Scripture warns us to *catch...the little foxes that ruin the vineyards.*[17] The following are "time bandits" we need to bring into captivity:

* Excessive television. The average American watches 19 hours a week. I used to stay up frequently and watch a lot of basketball games. While I would make no religious rule about it, I seldom do anymore. I simply ask myself, "Five years from now, what difference [especially in eternity] will it make if North Carolina or Virginia wins this ball game?!

* Excessive news. Some believers spend more time reading newspapers than they do their Bibles. It is good to be knowledgeable of world events, but we can waste a lot of time

reading negative and unnecessary information.

* Excessive talking. When Jesus sent out his disciples, he said, *do not greet anyone along the road.*[18] Jesus was not encouraging silence and rudeness, but the avoiding of long, protracted greetings characteristic of the oriental.[19] The disciples had a job to do and they needed to get on with it. Excessive talking can consume valuable time; some folks would rather talk about their problems than solve their problems God's way. *Let your words be few*[20] is still good advice for those who are the Lord's disciples.

* Excessive hobbies. There is certainly a place for recreation and hobbies, but a caution is in order: *"Everything is permissible for me"--but not everything is beneficial. "Everything is permissible for me"--but I will not be mastered by anything.*[21] The Living Bible says here, *Even if I am allowed to do them, I'll refuse to if I think they might get such a grip on me that I can't easily stop when I want to.* There are two sports that I personally cannot regularly participate in, because I know myself well enough to know they could easily "get a grip on me" and consume too much time. I also have developed a fascinating interest in the computer. The technology of our modern computers is quite incredible, but if I'm not careful, I could spend every spare hour at home pecking away or learning some new facet on my keyboard.

* Excessive sleep. Scripture says, *Do not <u>love</u> sleep...*[22] Our attitude should be to get only the <u>sleep that we need</u> -- no less and no more. Some people need more sleep than others. Women often seem to need more sleep than men. Whatever the case, our sleep should be under the lordship of Christ. When I first became a Christian I was convinced that I needed to sleep until seven o'clock every morning; after all, I had <u>always</u>

awakened at seven! Having a hunger for the word of God, I decided for a month I would start setting the alarm for ten minutes earlier and give God the first part of my morning. After the month it had become so natural to rise at 6:50, that I started trying 6:40. The extra ten minutes was a little harder to get used to, but I soon adapted. Today, many years later, I rise much earlier, but I have learned what my body needs. Sometimes the night before, I have to make a decision: Do I want to stay up until midnight watching a ball game or late movie, or is my proper sleep and time with God in the morning more important? I do stay up late occasionally, but this has become more the exception than the norm.

4. Take care of unpleasant tasks as soon as possible.

Procrastinators usually avoid taking action because (1) it is a difficult or unpleasant task or (2) it is possible they may not do a perfect job. Felix is a good example of a procrastinator:

> *And as he [Paul] was discussing righteousness, self-control, and the judgment to come, Felix became frightened and said, "Go away for the present, and when I find time, I will summon you.*[23]

Many of us have a problem with clutter. For every piece of paper one of three actions should take place: (1) throw it away, (2) act on it, or (3) file it away for reading or action at an appropriate time. You may think this is extreme, but I have learned in opening my mail to open the "junk" mail first and save the letters that I really want to read for last. This way I quickly can toss most mail and reduce my pile to things that are really important to me. On Saturdays if we make a list of things to do, why not do the most unpleasant jobs first, such as cleaning up the dog pen?

5. Learn to function even when you feel bad.

If we wait until we feel just right before we act, we will accomplish little in this life. The apostle Paul is our example of one who did not let the aches and pains of life slow him down; Paul was beaten black and blue, was shipwrecked, endured sleepless nights, suffered hunger, and among other things was given a "thorn in the flesh", a messenger of Satan sent to torment him. If any man ever needed a break, it was Paul! Yet he knew that God's grace was sufficient.

I have noticed over the years many flimsy excuses to avoid obedience to God and fellowship with his people. Christians sometimes will use a mere cold as an excuse to miss a Sunday gathering with the people of God. Or, if a baby causes a mother to miss a couple of hours of sleep, she may take that as an indication to "sleep in." We must consider our physical bodies, but we should not always let our physical bodies dictate to us and thereby hinder what God wants in our lives.

John Calvin (1509-1654) produced the greatest literary work to come out of the Reformation, The Institutes of Christian Religion, while suffering from constant headaches, spitting of blood, a hemorrhoidal vein (the pain of which increased to unbearable proportions because of an internal abscess that would not heal), intermittent fever, gallstones, kidney stones, stomach cramps, intestinal influenza, and arthritis.[24]

Richard Baxter (1615-1691), a puritan theologian, published 128 books (more than 35 thousand printed pages) and was renowned for his house-to-house ministry in Kidderminster, England, yet he was a walking museum of pathological conditions. He wrote, "I have these forty years been sensible to the sin of losing time; I could not spare an hour." He apologized for his books: "I wrote them in the crowd of all my other employments, in the midst of continual languishing and medicine, which would allow me no great leisure for polishing and exactness."[25]

We should have the same spirit as Caleb, who never let physical obstacles slow him down (see Num. 13-14). When eighty-five years old, instead of retiring and taking life easy, Caleb said, "*Now give me the hill country...the Anakites were there...but, the Lord helping me, I will drive them out just as he said.*"[26]

6. Discern between Divine interruptions and diversionary tactics of the enemy.

Billy Graham has become the world's leading evangelist because he concentrated on God's call of evangelism, refusing opportunities to be involved in political leadership or Christian education. Likewise, each one of us, after we know the will of God, needs to focus primarily on that calling and move toward the goal with all our hearts. The enemy of our souls is a master of diversionary tactics, as seen in his opposition to the work of Nehemiah:

> *Sanballat and Geshem sent me this message: "Come, let us meet together in one of the villages on the plain of Ono." But they were scheming to harm me; so I sent messengers to them with this reply: "I am carrying on a great project and cannot go down. Why should the work stop while I leave it and go down to you?" Four times they sent me the same message, and each time I gave them the same answer.*[27]

Nehemiah never gave Sanballat and Geshem the "time of day," because he realized they were there to distract from the work of God. I have noticed in my prayer time that sudden thoughts of details I have to do will pop into my mind. I keep a notepad always handy, so I can easily jot down notes, but I also have realized some of these diverting thoughts are from the devil himself, who hates anyone's spending intimate time with the Heavenly Father. A good prayer to regularly recite is, "Lord, keep me away from anything that would distract me from your good, perfect, and acceptable will."

7. Plan your week.

Plans are important, if they are flexible plans. Planning is not unspiritual and neither will it deny the Holy Spirit freedom to act:

> *We should make plans, counting on God to direct us.*[28]

> *The plans of the diligent lead to profit as surely as haste leads to poverty.*[29]

> *Don't go charging into battle without a plan.*[30]

To make no plans is a plan in itself. How many housewives know that a half-an-hour of meal planning can eliminate repeated trips to the store, reduce preparation time, minimize cost, and provide a better balanced diet? Crawford Greenwalt, former president of Dupont, once said, "One minute in planning saves three or four minutes in execution." In my own life I have been able to get the most accomplished when I have taken some time to plan. I don't feel bound to finish every list, but it helps me to make priorities. For example, if I have letters to write (a task which can easily be forgotten!), I will write a note in my schedule book on a particular day to "write letters." If I didn't schedule it, it probably wouldn't get done. Couples who want to obey the Scripture, *Practice hospitality*[31], will succeed better if they plan a get together at least 4-7 days in advance.

When I have a multitude of things to do on a Saturday, I will frequently take five minutes to list all my jobs with the most important ones highlighted. If I only get two or three done, I do not feel badly, because I've done the most important.

8. Finally, live life with a perspective of eternity.

> *So we fix our eyes not on what is seen, but on what is unseen. For what is seen is temporary, but what is unseen is eternal.*[32]

A motivating force which is seldom mentioned in time-management classes is a sense of eternity. Jonathan Edwards once prayed, "Lord, stamp eternity on my eyeballs." As believers we should have one underlying motivation for ordering our lives and trying to make our lives count in the kingdom of God -- one day we will have to stand before Almighty God and give an account of our actions (or lack of actions) as believers. This is not the great White Throne Judgment,[33] but an accounting of how we have used the talents God has entrusted to us.[34]

In Psalm 90 Moses has a perspective of eternity as he writes, *From everlasting to everlasting you are God...a thousand years in your sight are like a day that has just gone by...our days quickly pass, and we fly away...*[35] Moses' prayer in this psalm is certainly one we should make our own: *Teach us to order our days rightly, that we may enter the gate of wisdom.*[36]

NOTES

1.II Chron. 27:6 NAS

2.I Cor. 14:33

3.I Cor. 14:40 NAS with Greek translations in brackets

4.Col. 2:5 RSV

5.Joseph Thayer, Thayer's Greek-English Lexicon of the New Testament (Associated Publishers, Grand Rapids, MI)

6.These are adapted from an excellent book by Gordon MacDonald, Ordering Your Private World, (Oliver Nelson, Nashville, 1984) p. 65-67

7.Prov. 14:4 Living Bible

8.II Cor. 5:17

9.Billy Graham, Hope for the Troubled Heart (Word Publishing, Dallas, TX, 1991) p.200

10.Mk. 12:28-31

11.Matt. 6:33

12.Eph. 5:15-16 Phillips

13.J. Oswald Sanders, Spiritual Leadership (Moody Press, Chicago, IL, 1967) p.88

14.Quoted by Mark Porter in The Time of Your Life (Walterick Publishers, P.O. Box 2216, Kansas City, KS 66110) p.112. This is an excellent and very practical book on time management.

15.Moody Monthly, December 1989

16.Porter, p.5

17.Song of Sol. 2:15

18.Lk. 10:4

19.see Kenneth Wuest, The New Testament - An Expanded Translation (Eerdmans, Grand Rapids, MI, 1961) translation on Lk. 10:4

20.Ecc. 5:2

21.I Cor. 6:12

22.Prov. 20:13

23.Acts 24:25 NAS, emphasis mine

24.Porter, p.165

25.Ibid.,p.165

26.Josh. 14:10-12

27.Neh. 6:2-4

28.Prov. 16:9 Living Bible

29.Prov. 21:5
30.Prov. 20:18 Good News Bible
31.Rom. 12:13
32.II Cor. 4:18
33.Rev. 20:11-15
34.Matt 25:14-30; I Cor. 3:10-15; 4:5
35.Psa. 90:2,4,10
36.Psa. 90:12 New English Bible

Chapter Six

Making Room for the Holy Spirit

Frank does not have a very good relationship with his wife Sarah. He lives with her under the same roof, he makes constant use of her services, and he expects her to "be there" when he needs her. Frank, however, fails to communicate with Sarah, he seldom recognizes her presence, and he fails to enjoy her potential friendship. Frank's relationship with Sarah is lacking to say the least, yet it is very comparable to the relationship many believers have with the Holy Spirit.

Many of us agree in doctrine that the Holy Spirit is God and part of the Trinity. As far as knowing the person of the Holy Spirit and His working in practical ways is concerned, far too often our knowledge is limited. To some the Holy Spirit is just a theological concept or an impersonal "force." For others who believe in the Holy Spirit, the *fellowship of the Holy Spirit*

(II Cor. 13:14; Phil 2:1) is often not a reality. Fellowship with the Holy Spirit means we personally commune with the Holy Spirit. Instead of treating the Holy Spirit as a waiter in a restaurant, we need to invite His presence, His anointing, His leading, and His comfort. Whenever we read the Scripture we should invite the Holy Spirit to teach us; we should never assume that we will learn anything without His revelation to our hearts.[1]

In this chapter, we cannot cover the comprehensive teaching of the Holy Spirit. There are important topics as the baptism of the Holy Spirit, the fruits of the Holy Spirit, and walking in the Holy Spirit. Our focus, however, is simply on giving the Holy Spirit rightful place.

God's Desire to Dwell Among Us

When God came to earth, His primary purpose was <u>not</u> just to "save" man; He has always desired to have a people with whom he could <u>dwell</u>: *the Word became flesh and dwelt among us.*[2] The Greek word for "dwell" in the above verse actually means "tabernacled." In other words, God desires to pitch His tent with us! This truth was stated long ago when God gave His law to Moses:

> *Moreover, I will make my dwelling among you and My soul will not reject you. I will also walk among you and be your God, and you shall be My people.*[3]

We see from cover to cover in the Bible God's desire to dwell among us . In the Old Covenant God chose Zion, the Jewish people, because he desired them *for his dwelling.*[4] In the New Covenant we see God's focus of attention on His church, which is not declared to be a mere "teaching center", a place where "needs are met," or an organization which tries to keep

Christians happy. No, rather His called-out-ones are first and foremost intended to be the home of God; we are *being built together to become a dwelling in which God lives by his Spirit.*[5] In the final chapters of God's record, we see His ultimate desire for His people, His bride, the New Jerusalem:

> *And I heard a loud voice from the throne saying, "Now the dwelling of God is with men, and he will live with them. They will be his people, and God himself will be with them and be their God.*[6]

T. Austin-Sparks, a Bible teacher who had much insight into the body of Christ, was quite honest about a major weakness he saw among evangelical believers:

> The writer, over a period of nearly forty years of personal contact with evangelical Christianity in many parts of the world, has been terribly impressed with one basic weakness or defect;...While the <u>doctrine</u> of the Holy Spirit is well known...there is a great deal to make real the question if ...the majority of Christians know anything about the Holy Spirit as a positive, active, indwelling presence.[7]

A dwelling place is what God is after. Certainly salvation from an eternity in hell is part of God's plan, but it is not His full purpose. If a house is on fire and a fire truck comes and puts out the fire and saves the house, has the purpose of the house been fulfilled? No! A house is intended to be a <u>dwelling place</u>. It is also one thing to be a visitor in a house and quite another thing to feel completely at home in a house. When I feel completely at home (in my own house) I can kick off my shoes, rearrange furniture, and look in any closet I please.

If I am visiting in a house, however, I do not feel freedom to do any of those things. If this matter of the indwelling Christ was not a deficiency in the lives of believers, the apostle Paul would not have prayed as he did:

> *...that He would grant to you...to be strengthened through the Spirit in the inward man, that Christ might finally settle down and feel completely at home in your hearts...*[8]

The Holy Spirit as Initiator

The book of Acts is not to be thought of as merely the acts of the apostles; rather this book of early church history is the record of the acts of the Holy Spirit through the apostles. The Holy Spirit appears throughout this book and we can quickly conclude that He, and not man, is the initiator of what God accomplished through the disciples.
J. I. Packer states it well:

> The Christian's life in all its aspects -- intellectual and ethical, devotional and relational, upsurging in worship and outgoing in witness -- is supernatural; only the Spirit can initiate and sustain it.[9]

The book of Acts reveals the Holy Spirit, not man, as the great initiator in the work of His church. Consider the following:

* It was the Holy Spirit, who birthed the first church (Acts 2).
* It was the Holy Spirit who empowered the first spokesman (preacher) of the early church (Acts 4:8).

* It was the Holy Spirit who gave believers the boldness to share their faith in Christ (Acts 4:31).
* It was the Holy Spirit who brought conviction and conversion to the first Gentile converts (Acts 10:44-45).
* It was the Holy Spirit (not a church board) who set apart the first missionary team (Acts 13:1-2).
* It was the Holy Spirit who helped the apostles decide a major debate among the Christians (Acts 15:28).
* It was the Holy Spirit who decided the apostles' itineraries (Acts 16:6-7).
* It was the Holy Spirit who chose elders in local churches (Acts 20:28).

One of the believer's greatest temptations is to neglect the Holy Spirit and "take matters into our own hands." C.T. Studd, a man quite familiar with mission work, commented:

> How little chance the Holy Ghost has nowadays. The churches and missionary societies have so bound Him in red tape that they practically ask Him to sit in a corner while they do the work themselves.[10]

God's children are not those who dictate to God, but rather those who are *led by the Spirit.*[11] We are warned not to *resist the Holy Spirit*[12], not to *grieve the Holy Spirit*[13], not to *insult* the Holy Spirit[14], and not to *quench the Spirit.*[15] We can quench the Spirit in another believer or in ourselves. In a sense, we "pour cold water" on the Spirit when we become critical and resentful of others or stifle the prompting of the Spirit in ourselves. One version says, *Never damp the fire of the Spirit.*[16]

The book of Galatians was written to warn believers against neglecting the Holy Spirit and reverting into man-made traditions and self-efforts:

> *Are you so foolish? After beginning with the Spirit, are you now trying to attain your goal by human effort?*[17]

God's words to Zerubbabel still speak loudly today:

> *"Not by might nor by power, but by my Spirit," says the Lord Almighty.*[18]

This Scripture should apply to our own personal accomplishments that are done in the name of the Lord, as well as the work of the corporate church. M. Lloyd-Jones makes a valid point:

> When the church operates in the power and strength of the Holy Spirit, it does more in one day than it would otherwise do through all its activities without the Spirit in years.[19]

A good test of how much church work depends on the Holy Spirit or only on man is this simple test: how well would this work do if this certain man were gone? If it "falls to pieces", then possibly the work is on a faulty foundation. A. W. Tozer puts it even more bluntly:

> You can write it down as a fact: no matter what a man does, no matter how successful he seems to be in any field, if the Holy Spirit is not the chief energizer of his activity, it will all fall apart when he dies.[20]

Robert Girard suggests a principle which probably would not be welcomed today in many churches, but it would certainly contribute to the spiritual depth of any local body who practiced it:

> Anything in the church program that cannot be maintained without constant pastoral pressure on the people should be allowed to die a sure and natural death.[21]

Flexibility is Needed

Planning is certainly not against Scripture. We are exhorted to love God *with all our mind*[22] and to *make plans, counting on God to direct us.*[23] Our plans, however, both for ourselves and for the church should be flexible. There are pastors who plan out their messages four months in advance, more dictated by events on a calendar than the revealing of the real need by the Holy Spirit. I have visited quite a number of churches (both "charismatic" and "non-charismatic"), and in most Sunday morning meetings, there is little flexibility in the format. Usually songs, Scripture readings, announcements, and sermon are so well planned that even if the Holy Spirit wanted to do something different, He couldn't! Church leaders might justify this in the name of "order" or say that the Holy Spirit led them to make all their plans during the week. Michael Green, British theologian and evangelist, shares his impression:

> Most modern churches...don't need to be told that worship is ordered. They know it very well. It is often tightly shut, so tight that nobody could take part in it if it had not been prearranged, let alone the Holy Spirit.[24]

The New Testament idea of church meetings was quite different from most modern day meetings. In giving specific direction for church meetings, Paul encourages all to come prepared to contribute, not just to sit as spectators, while a few "professionals" perform. Every believer may potentially have something which could edify the others, whether it be a testimony, a teaching, a scripture reading, a song, or a prophetic word.[25] Paul is clear that the service should be orderly and not confusing[26], but he also encourages flexibility:

> *But should a message of truth come to one who is seated, then the original speaker should stop talking. For in this way you can all have the opportunity to give a message, one after the other, and everyone will learn something and everyone will have his faith stimulated.*[27]

For the past ten years I have shared the pastoral leadership with a few other men in a church about 250-300 in size. If you ever visit you will hopefully discover two things very quickly: (1) we are far from being a perfect church, and (2) because of His unfathomable love and patience, God dwells among us. Our meetings are planned since we have an organized worship team and structured teaching from gifted men. However, in all our planning we want to give the body of Christ an opportunity to respond if the Holy Spirit nudges them. In most meetings we have some "open time" for anyone to contribute as the Spirit leads. We usually do not have to wait long; someone will bring a Scripture, someone else will give a testimony of God's protection of a child, and yet another will share an emotional struggle and request prayer. There have also been a few times in which the above verse became a reality; on some occasions there were so many edifying words coming from different believers, that the planned message was "put on hold" until another meeting. The Holy Spirit in such times just seemed to "take over" with His own agenda. Oswald Chambers once said,

"God takes great delight in breaking up our programs."[28] This type of meeting is quite risky for us who shepherd the flock, but we do not feel the meeting belongs to us. Sometimes we do have "off-the-wall" things happen or awkward times of silence. However, the good far outweighs the bad, and the group has been blessed by this kind of format.

Probably one of the most needed charismatic gifts of the Holy Spirit in our day, if we are willing to make room for it, is the gift of *piloting*. This may not be a recognizable gift at first, but it is listed in I Cor. 12:28 where most translations either translate it *gifts of administration* (NIV and NAS) or *governments* (KJ). The Greek word, however, means "a pilot, one who steers a ship." (The same word is used in Acts 27:11 of a pilot.) If our meetings are truly going to be led by the Holy Spirit, men will be used whose lives are *hidden with Christ in God*[29], who are gifted to "pilot" a meeting, guiding and steering in the appropriate direction. This will not be a singular leader as the gift is listed in the plural. A man with this gift may be an elder, a worship leader, or just an "ordinary" brother. Whoever they are, these persons will be willing to step forward and provide direction as the Spirit prompts. One modern Bible version translated this gift as *power...to direct*[30] Another translator says, *power...to guide.*[31] Gerhard Kittle, in his exhaustive Greek dictionary, makes this comment:

> The reference can only be to the specific gifts which qualify a Christian to be a helmsman to his congregation, i.e., a true director of its order and therewith of its life.[32]

God will use some with the gift of piloting in guiding the general affairs of the church -- i.e., in "steering" the group in a specific direction. This gift, like any gift of the Holy Spirit, should not just be limited to the context of church meetings.

Every congregation, however, which desires the Holy Spirit to orchestrate its meetings, should pray earnestly for God to raise up several brothers who have this gift of piloting.

Flexibility in Personal Decisions

In our American society of vast organization and detailed time schedules, flexibility does not always come easily. Someone has defined flexible as "willing to change with a happy spirit." The last part of the definition is the key for the believer. If the Lord is dealing with us and we make changes, but still harbor a resentful or bitter attitude in our hearts, we are grieving the Holy Spirit. I have known estranged husbands and wives who were willing to change behavior patterns and habits, but unless they have had a change of heart through repentance, the marriage problems have only been complicated.

The flexible man must be willing to be inconvenienced. It seems that most opportunities to serve others do not come at ideal times. Tozer relates a very solemn incident:

> I heard of a certain man of God who had been greatly used in praying for the sick with the natural result that he was often called out at very inopportune times and under circumstances that were anything but pleasant. Once when sent for in the middle of the night he threw himself across the bed and complained to God the lack of consideration the call evinced. That was the end for him. Thereafter no one was ever delivered in answer to his prayer, even though he sought with many tears to capture again the gift he had lost.[33]

The apostle Paul was a man of plans but also a flexible man. In Acts 16 Paul and his fellow workers planned to visit Asia to preach the gospel in uncharted lands, but they were *kept by the Holy Spirit.* Then, when they subsequently planned to travel to Bithynia, *the Spirit of Jesus would not allow them to.* Following this, God gave a vision and instructed the team to travel to Macedonia.[34] Paul was a man of carefully planned action, but he was also a man who could be interrupted by the Holy Spirit.

The Spirit of God is soverign and will do as He pleases. We cannot put Him in our own mold. In the Bible, most of the symbols of the Holy Spirit are fluid -- wind, oil, fire, and water. We cannot hold these in our hands. We must realize (as soon as possible) that God will not allow us to "fence Him in."

Flexibility is needed in our personal lives as several biblical illustrations reveal:

* **Flexible wineskins** are required to handle the "new wine" (see Lk. 5:37-38). If the wineskins are not fresh and flexible, they will crack and the good wine will be spilled out.

* **Flexible clay** is required in the hands of the potter (see Jer. 18:1-6). If clay is not flexible (moldable), it will soon become hard and brittle, useless to the potter.

* **Flexible air currents** depict the believer; Jesus said that everyone born of the Spirit (not just some far-out mystics) would be like the wind: *the wind blows where it wishes and you hear the sound of it, but do not know where it comes from or where it is going.*[35] This is not to imply that we need to be unstable or "flighty." However, we are challenged to *be on the alert*[36], ready to change direction.

* **Flexible palm trees** also describe the believer (Psa. 92:14;

Song of Sol. 7:7). Palm trees more than any other tree can withstand storm winds. There are two reasons for this; one is that palm trees have a massive, thick root system and second, palm trees are flexible, they bend with the wind.

Personal flexibility is essential for personal growth. Probably none of us relishes uncertainty but some of it is unavoidable in the Spirit-filled life. DeVern Fromke comments:

> Where there is no continuous governing of the Holy Spirit, whether in our personal walk or ministry, or in our church services or fellowship, there will be no real development of inner stature. Inward spiritual growth comes only as the believer or group gladly responds to the daily, fresh breath of the Spirit intending to govern the life. The result is a continuous inward stretching, adjusting and enlarging.[37]

If left to go our own way, we tend to get settled, *like wine left to settle undisturbed and never poured from jar to jar.*[38] It was customary in Bible times to pour wine from one jar to another to improve the quality and separate the good liquid from the sediment and scum. This process was done, as many times as necessary, until the purity and sweetness were enough to satisfy the owner. Although none of us enjoys the "unsettling of the Holy Spirit," it is for greater fruitfulness in our lives. Wine allowed to settle and ferment for a long time forms a hard crust and becomes syrupy, bitter, and unpalatable.

Waiting Upon God

The crucial thing is to *keep in step with the Spirit.*[39] We should avoid two extremes: *to not be like the horse*, who tends to run on ahead, *nor to be like the mule,*[40] who tends to stick his heels in and lag behind. We simply need to wait upon God and move when He moves. The generation of Israelites in Moses' day learned this lesson in a vivid way; the Lord's cloud would hover over their camp and when the cloud moved, they would break camp and move after it. If the cloud stopped for a few days or a few months, they would stop, too.[41] In our fast-paced, instant-oriented society, we are used to getting things done right now, without delay; therefore, waiting upon God "goes against our grain." God, however, will move mightily for the one who has learned to wait on Him:

> *For from old they have not heard nor perceived by ear, neither has the eye seen a God besides Thee, who acts in behalf of the one who waits for Him.*[42]
>
> *Wait for the LORD and keep his way. He will exalt you to inherit the land...*[43]
>
> *The Lord longs to be gracious to you...*
> *Blessed are all who wait for him.*[44]

Waiting on God doesn't mean "mindless-Christianity" or passivity. Francis Schaeffer explains:

> Let us not think that waiting on the Lord will mean getting less done. The truth is that by doing the Lord's work in the Lord's way we will accomplish more, not less. You need not fear that if you wait for God's Spirit you will not get as much done as if you charge ahead in the flesh. After all, who can do the most, you or the God of heaven and earth?[45]

Waiting upon God means we give God opportunity to speak, direct, or act before we "plow right on ahead." Many mistakes of God's people would have been avoided if they had only given God some time. Joshua, a man who certainly followed the Lord wholeheartedly[46], made a mistake, however, when he made a peace treaty with the neighboring Gibeonites, who had disguised themselves as far-away travelers. This mistake with its ongoing consequences occurred because *the chief men...did not at first seek guidance from the Lord.*[47] Sometimes in our church "business meetings" we elders and deacons have been reproved by the Lord for neglecting Him in prayer. We realize it is so easy for us to give a ten second "Lord, bless our plans" prayer and jump right into business. We know we should take more time for prayer, especially at the beginning of such meetings, and wait on the Lord. The Holy Spirit should indeed have room even in our church "business meetings." In an early church meeting in which some practical and controversial matters were discussed, the leaders were able to say in the end, "*It seemed good to the Holy Spirit and to us...*"[48]

In conclusion, let us consider this word from Andrew Murray's excellent devotional book, <u>Waiting on God</u>:

> If we truly set ourselves to wait upon God, we shall find that it is with Him we are impatient, because He does not at once, or as soon as we could wish, do our bidding. It is in waiting upon God that our eyes are opened to believe in His wise and sovereign will, and to see that the sooner and the more completely we yield absolutely to it, the more surely His blessing can come to us...
>
> All the exercises of the spiritual life, our reading and praying, our willing and doing, have

their very great value. But they can go no farther than this, that they point the way and prepare us in humility to look and depend upon God Himself, and in patience to wait His good time and mercy. The waiting is to teach us our absolute dependence upon God's mighty working, and to make us in perfect patience place ourselves at His disposal. They that wait on the Lord shall inherit the land; the promised land and its blessing. The heirs must wait; they can afford to wait.[49]

NOTES

1.see Jn. 14:26. Anytime we approach Scripture, it should not be as any other book. We should come humbly and ask the Holy Spirit to teach us personally His truth for this day. Apart from the Holy Spirit, the Bible will not be understood (I Cor. 2:14). Two good prayers to address to the Holy Spirit as we read the Word are Psa. 119:18 and Eph. 1:17.

2.Jn. 1:14 NAS

3.Lev. 26:11-12 NAS

4.Psa. 132:13

5.Eph. 2:22

6.Rev. 21:3

7.T. Austin-Sparks, Words of Wisdom and Revelation (Three Brothers, Box 409, Corinna, ME) p. 37

8.Eph. 3:17 translation by Kenneth Wuest, The New Testament: An Expanded Translation (Eerdmans, Grand Rapids, MI,1961)

9.J.I.Packer, Keep in Step With the Spirit (Fleming Revell, Old Tappan, NJ, 1984) p.9

10.Jean Walker, Fool and Fanatic (World Evangelization Crusade, 1980) p.120

11.Rom. 8:14

12.Acts 7:51

13.Eph. 4:30

14.Heb. 10:29

15.I Thes. 5:19 NAS

16.I Thes. 5:19 Phillips

17.Gal. 3:3

18.Zech. 4:6

19.D.M. Lloyd-Jones, Knowing the Times (Banner of Truth Trust, Carlisle, PA, 1989) p.30

20.Harry Verploegh, A.W. Tozer -- An Anthology (Christian Publications, Camp Hill, PA, 1984) p. 114

21.Robert Girard, Brethren, Hang Loose! (Zondervan, Grand Rapids, MI, 1972) p.73

22.Lk. 10:27

23.Prov. 16:9 Living Bible

24.Michael Green, Evangelism Through the Local Church (Thomas Nelson Pub., Nashville, TN, 1990) p.105

25.I Cor. 14:26

26.I Cor. 14:33,40

27.I Cor. 14:30-31 Phillips

28.Harry Verploegh, Oswald Chambers: The Best From All His Books (Thomas Nelson, Nashville, TN, 1987) p. 273

29.Col. 3:3

30.I Cor. 12:28 Good News Bible

31.I Cor. 12:28 Revised English Bible

32.Gerhard Kittle, Theological Dictionary of the New Testament (Eerdmans, Grand Rapids, MI, 1965) p.1036

33.A. W. Tozer, Of God and Men (Christian Publications, Harrisburg, PA, 1960) p.93

34.Acts 16:6-10

35.Jn. 3:8

36.e.g. Eph. 6:18; I Thes. 5:6

37.DeVern Fromke, Unto Full Stature (Sure Foundation Ministries, Indianapolis, IN, 1964) p. 199

38.Jer. 48:11 Good News Bible

39.Gal. 5:25

40.Psa. 32:9

41.Num. 9:15-23

42.Is. 64:4 NAS

43.Psa. 37:34

44.Is. 30:18

45.Francis Schaeffer, No Little People (InterVarsity Press, Downers Grove, IL) p. 72

46.Num. 14:8

47.Josh. 9:14 NEB

48.Acts 15:28

49.Andrew Murray, Waiting on God (Moody Press, Chicago, IL, 1982) p. 60-61

Chapter Seven

Maintaining Hope for the Future

Richard Baxter, an English Puritan leader in the seventeenth century was chronically sick and had plenty of reason to be a miserable man in his life. Tubercular from his teens, Baxter suffered constantly from indigestion, kidney stones, headaches, toothaches, swollen limbs, internal bleeding, and all this before the days of pain-relieving drugs. In spite of his physical condition, Baxter was outgoing, energetic, and uncomplaining. By 1661 he had evangelized his entire town of Kidderminster, which had a population of two thousand adults plus children. Baxter also wrote regularly, producing some classic devotional books which are still used by many Christians today. In one of these books, The Saint's Everlasting Rest, he tells his secret. From his thirtieth year he practiced a habit which he began when he thought he was about to die: for about a half an hour a day Baxter would meditate on the life to come and the glories awaiting him. This practice instilled hope in his heart and gave this servant the motivation and strength to keep on going. Hope for the future made the difference in the life of Richard Baxter and it can make a difference in our lives as well.

Probably one of the most neglected and misunderstood of all Biblical words is the word "hope." Hope, if properly understood and implanted in our minds, is something that can make disciples of Christ confident, encouraged, motivated, and able to smile at the future. Hope is one of three abiding realities along with faith and love: Scripture says, *There are three things that last for ever: faith, hope, and love.*[1] Christian bookstores usually have dozens of book titles on subjects related to faith and love, but how often do we see books or hear sermons on hope?

Before we met Christ, we were *without hope in this world.*[2] After we encounter Christ and surrender our lives to His lordship, we are *born again into a life full of hope.*[3] When we are subsequently filled with the Holy Spirit, one reason for this empowering from above is to make us radiant with hope:

> *May the God of hope fill you with all joy and peace in your faith, that by the power of the Holy Spirit, your whole life and outlook may be radiant with hope.*[4]

Today mankind is in tremendous spiritual conflict and much of that spiritual warfare takes place in the mind. Most of our basic problems affect the mind: worry, depression, stress, and fear. However, God has not left us without a remedy; in Ephesians 6 we are instructed to *take the helmet of salvation.*[5] In another passage, Paul is more specific; he calls this helmet the *hope of salvation.*[6] A helmet protects the mind, and if we "put on" hope, it will protect against many mental dangers. Our minds will thereby be more fit to serve the purposes of God.

Our Definition Makes a Difference

How we define "hope" can make the difference between a weak, theological concept and a life-producing force. Here is a good, simple definition for those who know the Lord:

> Hope is the continued, mental expectation of good; a settled confidence that God has good plans for our future:

This definition is supported by the prophet Jeremiah:

> *For I know the plans I have for you, declares the LORD, plans to prosper you and not to harm you, plans to give you hope and a future.*[7]

Biblical hope is not the same as our current English usage, e.g., "I hope so!" For many who express this kind of vague hope, the words are only empty. Jack Hayford says it well:

> For most people you meet, hope is a "cross-my-fingers" kind of thing shot through with guesswork. Instead, for the believer, hope is *divinely assured things that aren't here yet!* Our hope is grounded in unshakable promises...[8]

One Biblical analogy compares hope to an anchor:

> *We have this hope as an anchor for the soul, firm and secure.*[9]

Our hope in the Lord and His plans for our future is something sure and steadfast. Why does a boat need an anchor? Because it is designed to float in water and water is a totally unstable element. Derek Prince expands this idea:

> There's nothing in water to give stability, so if the boat is to be stable, it must have an anchor which passes from the ship through the water to some other element, such as a rock, which is stable. Once the anchor is fastened to the stable element, then the boat is stabilized.....
>
> You and I are like that boat. We live in an element that is totally unstable ..... Neither money nor real estate nor anything else that we look at can give us stability ..... If we want stability, we must have an anchor that passes out of time into eternity. When our anchor is fastened upon the eternal presence of Almighty God, we are *secure* ..... What is that anchor? *Hope.....*[10]

Hope is different from faith although the two words are closely related. Faith deals more with the present; hope deals more with the future:

> *If it is for this life only that Christ has given us hope, we of all people are most to be pitied.*[11]

Faith brings the promises of God into present reality, whereas hope awaits for future fulfillment. Scripture says, *Now faith is...*[12], indicating that faith operates more in the present. This is not to say that faith will always receive an answer in this lifetime.[13] Some Christians are disappointed because they only live for the present and fail to hope for the future. Scripture says, *Hope that is seen is no hope at all. Who hopes for what he already has?*[14] Judson Cornwall points out an interesting fact about hope:

> Hope is never attributed to Jesus, nor did the word ever cross his lips except for the occasion when he referred to "your hope." For Him the realities of the next world and of the future were so completely familiar that He did not need hope. [15]

What Hope Will Do For Us

1. Hope in the Lord will keep us from being discouraged; it will lift us up and keep us going when all natural circumstances tell us to quit.

Many of God's "heroes of faith" probably felt like quitting at times, but hope kept them going. Consider these well-known men of God:

> * Job lost his family, his possessions, and his health, but he put his trust in God, boldly declaring, *Though He slay me, I will hope in Him...*[16]
>
> * Abraham faced an "impossible" task of producing a son in old age, yet *Abraham, human reason for hope being gone, hoped on in faith...*[17]
>
> * Paul, on a boat facing certain shipwreck in a hurricane, refused to be daunted by natural circumstances and exclaimed, "*Keep up your courage, men, for I believe God, that it will turn out exactly as I have been told.*"[18]

2. Hope in the Lord will keep us happy when we have every reason to be sad.

One of the great testimonies of Christian people to this world is that they can maintain a deep, inner joy when on the surface they should have every reason to be miserable and depressed. Only hope can make the difference. Scripture says, *Be joyful in hope.*[19] Hope will put a song in the heart. The prophet Hosea said,

> *I will make...the valley of Achor a door of hope. There she will sing as in the days of her youth...*[20]

This is not speaking of trite, outward happiness; happiness is so often related to "what is happening" around us. Joy, on the other hand, is much deeper; it comes from the Lord and does not rise and fall because of circumstances.

The word "Achor" in the above verse means "trouble" or "disaster" in the Hebrew language. In disastrous situations we can place our hope in God. Some believers in disastrous situations wring their hands and act as heathens who do not know the living God. Our times of trouble can become a door of hope. Most of the psalms were songs or poems written not in a comfortable air-conditioned study, but rather in the midst of very distressing settings. One psalmist, feeling "down-in-the-dumps," encouraged himself:

> *Why are you downcast, O my soul? Why so disturbed within me? Put your hope in God, for I will yet praise him...*[21]

3. Hope in the Lord will give us new strength.

> *Those who hope in the LORD will renew their strength. They will soar on wings like eagles; they will run and not grow weary, they will walk and not be faint.*[22]

If we truly hope in the Lord, we will do more than just "renew" our strength. The Hebrew word can also mean "exchange." In other words, we literally exchange our weak strength for <u>God's</u> strength. This is a thrilling promise, for when we exchange our strength for His, it's like exchanging a flashlight battery for the "power plant of heaven"! Then we can begin to move again...*to run and not grow weary and to walk and not faint.* In Hebrew it says we *sprout wings like eagles.* This means that hope produces new growth, new vision, and new God-given ability.

Regardless of age, we can have a youthful spirit restored. King David, who certainly knew personally the "wears and tears" of life, even in his prime years, declared:

> *He...satisfies your desires with good things so that your youth is renewed like the eagle's.*[23]

I have read that certain eagles live to be a hundred years old, but sometime around fifty or sixty they begin to mope around and no longer seem interested in riding the air currents. They do not seem to care if its raining or snowing and have little interest in "fellowship" with other eagles. But after some time of this, the older eagle will suddenly start beating his wings on a rock, knock off chunks of overgrown cartilage on his beak, and rub his tail feathers against the rocks until he looks "bruised and beat." As the old feathers are lost, however, new feathers begin to grow. The beak becomes sharp and more usable. The tail feathers grow out more thickly and beautifully, and soon the old bird has taken on the appearance of a young bird. The eagle has "renewed his youth" and is good for many more years. May this analogy be true for all "eagle Christians" who hope in the Lord.

4. Hope in the Lord will keep us praying and optimistic concerning backsliders or those in downtrodden conditions.

> *At least there is hope for a tree: If it is cut down, it will sprout again, and its new shoots will not fail.*[24]

We all know some "trees" that have been "cut down." In some cases the plunge has taken place because of one's own sin and stubbornness. In other cases it may be the chastening hand of the Lord or possibly the destructive work of Satan, the enemy of our souls. Whatever the case, we who hope in the Lord are optimistic: *it will sprout again!* Sometimes when people are in pathetic conditions, it may be hard to have faith for them. However, with the mercy of God, we can have hope. God is not willing for <u>any</u> to perish, but for <u>all</u> to come to repentance.[25]

This word of hope also applies to church groups which seem to have fallen short of God's intention. It is quite easy to become pessimistic about the church, but if a group of believers humble themselves, repent, and earnestly seek the face of God, there is hope! These believers can *wake up and strengthen what remains.*[26]

Hope will keep us patiently praying for the "impossible cases."

> *But if we hope for what we do not yet have, we wait for it patiently.*[27]

And hope does not disappoint us, because God has poured out his love into our hearts by the Holy Spirit, whom he has given us.[28]

How To Obtain Greater Hope

Any idea of hope that is not founded in the resurrected Christ who desires to indwell every believer is a false hope. Mere optimism or positive confession is not enough; these can become deceptive religious exercises if our lives are not truly anchored in Christ, the Solid Rock.[29] The great mystery of the ages is *Christ in you, the hope of glory.*[30] Scripture exhorts us to *base your happiness on your hope in Christ.*[31] Apart from Jesus, there is no real hope whatsoever, and a false hope can be a dangerous thing, as A. W. Tozer points out:

> The hope, for instance, which almost all people feel, of long life here on earth, can be for many a deadly snare, a fatal delusion. The average man, when he thinks of his future, suspends reason, falls back on unreasoning hope and creates for himself an expectation of peaceful and unnumbered days yet to come. This blind optimism works all right till the last day, that inevitable last day which comes to all; then it betrays the victim into the pit from which there is no escape...The big thing is to be sure we are not lulled to sleep by a false hope, that we do not waste our time dreaming about days that are not to be ours.[32]

As we therefore look at these practical measures in obtaining greater hope in our souls, we must realize they are all rooted in a vital relationship with Jesus Christ:

1. Let us meditate on God's great love and faithfulness.

Because of the unfathomable love of God and his faithfulness in the midst of our unfaithfulness, we can make it! Instead of dwelling primarily on our shortcomings and limitations, we need to dwell more on these attributes of God.

> *Yet this I call to mind and therefore I have hope: Because of the Lord's great love we are not consumed, for his compassions never fail. They are new every morning; great is your faithfulness.*[33]

2. Let us abide in the Scriptures.

Without time reading, studying, and meditating on the Scriptures, we will have little help for ourselves or for others that need our assistance. Any good intentions will only fall short if our lives are not rooted in the Word.

> *For everything that was written in the past was written to teach us, so that through endurance and the encouragement of the Scriptures we might have hope.*[34]

A major purpose of the written word of God is to produce hope in our hearts. Whenever I meet believers who are complaining, I usually ask them in the course of conversation if they have been abiding in Scripture and spending time with their Heavenly Father. With few exceptions, the reply is negative.

3. Let us confess our optimism and expectancy in God's plan for the future.

Make our future as happy as our past was sad.[35]

We need to guard what comes out of our mouths. If we have hope in our hearts, we should speak forth hope. If we have suffered greatly, the above verse should be an encouragement. Some of us may have to endure unpleasant circumstances for a while -- physical pain, a bad job, or an uncaring mate. Regardless of the conditions, we can echo words of hope like the following:

> *But as for me, I will always have hope; I will praise you more and more. My mouth will tell of your righteousness, of your salvation all day long, though I know not its measure. I will come and proclaim your mighty acts, O Sovereign LORD; I will proclaim your righteousness, yours alone.*[36]

We are not talking here of blind optimism or looking through "rose colored glasses" at what's coming upon the earth. But if all that comes out of our mouths is complaining, moaning, and negative talk, it is a sure sign we do not have much hope in the Lord. If we are truly confident that God is faithful and has plans for our future, our speech will reflect it. As one brother has said, if Romans 8:28 is true, then no believer should be a pessimist! Even if bleak circumstances never improve while we live out our days on this earth, Scripture says we can *rejoice in the hope of the glory of God.*[37] The Living Bible is more descriptive here: *we confidently and joyfully look forward to actually becoming all that God has had in mind for us to be.*[38]

In the stormy times of life let us put our "anchors" into Jesus, the Solid Rock. He is unshakable, immovable, utterly stable and absolutely secure. Let us resist the enemy, put on the helmet of hope, and earnestly reaffirm our confidence in our mighty God who has good things in store for those who hope in Him; let us say to our souls:

> *O my soul...put your hope in God, for I will yet praise him, my Savior and my God.*[39]

NOTES

1.I Cor. 13:13 New English Bible

2.Eph. 2:12

3.I Pet. 1:3 Phillips

4.Rom. 15:13 Phillips

5.Eph. 6:17

6.I Thes. 5:8

7.Jer. 29:11

8.Jack Hayford, Moments With Majesty (Multnomah Press, Portland, OR, 1990) p.50

9.Heb. 6:19

10.Derek Prince, article "War on the Mind" in New Wine Magazine, March 1983 (Integrity Communications, Mobile, AL)

11.I Cor. 15:19 Revised English Bible

12.Heb. 11:1

13.e.g. Heb. 11:39

14.Rom. 8:24

15.Judson Cornwall, Unfeigned Faith (Fleming Revell Co., Old Tappan, NJ, 1981) p. 44

16.Job 13:15

17.Rom. 4:18 The Amplified Bible

18.Acts 27:25 NAS

19.Rom. 12:12

20.Hos. 2:15

21.Psa. 42:5

22.Is. 40:31

23.Psa. 103:5

24.Job. 14:7

25.II Pet. 3:9

26.Rev. 3:2

27.Rom. 8:25

28.Rom. 5:5

29.Positive confession in itself can lead to false hope and deceive those who are not personally acquainted with the Lord or obedient to His revealed will. See Jer. 37:9 NAS; Ecc. 7:23; Matt 6:7 and Ezek. 13:6 (New English Bible says here, *They expect their words to control the event.*)

30.Col. 1:27

31.Rom. 12:12 Phillips

32.A.W. Tozer, We Travel an Appointed Way (Christian Publications, Camp Hill, PA,1988) p.84-86

33.Lam. 3:21-23

34.Rom 15:4

35.Psa. 90:15 Jerusalem Bible

36.Psa. 71:14-16

37.Rom. 5:2

38.Rom. 5:2 Living Bible

39.Psa. 42:5